PIANO/VOCAL/GUITAR – THE VERY BEST OF SHERYL CROW

2 ALL I WANNA DO

10 SOAK UP THE SUN

18 MY FAVORITE MISTAKE

24 THE FIRST CUT IS THE DEEPEST

30 EVERYDAY IS A WINDING ROAD

36 LEAVING LAS VEGAS

48 STRONG ENOUGH

43 LIGHT IN YOUR EYES

52 IF IT MAKES YOU HAPPY

57 THE DIFFICULT KIND

64 PICTURE

68 STEVE MCQUEEN

74 A CHANGE WOULD DO YOU GOOD

78 HOME

88 THERE GOES THE NEIGHBORHOOD

83 I SHALL BELIEVE

ISBN 978-1-5400-7077-7

For all works contained herein:
Unauthorized copying, arranging, adapting, recording, Internet posting, public performance,
or other distribution of the music in this publication is an infringement of copyright.
Infringers are liable under the law.

Visit Hal Leonard Online at
www.halleonard.com

Contact us:
Hal Leonard
7777 West Bluemound Road
Milwaukee, WI 53213
Email: info@halleonard.com

In Europe, contact:
Hal Leonard Europe Limited
42 Wigmore Street
Marylebone, London, W1U 2RN
Email: info@halleonardeurope.com

In Australia, contact:
Hal Leonard Australia Pty. Ltd.
4 Lentara Court
Cheltenham, Victoria, 3192 Australia
Email: info@halleonard.com.au

ALL I WANNA DO

Words and Music by KEVIN GILBERT,
DAVID BAERWALD, SHERYL CROW,
WYN COOPER and BILL BOTTRELL

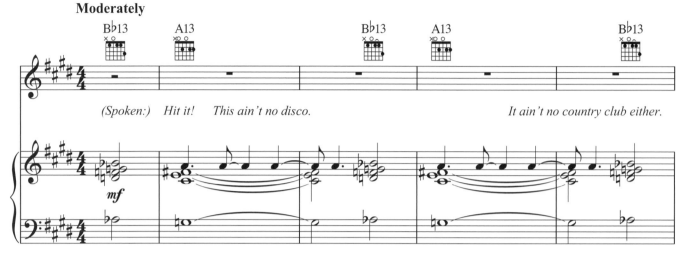

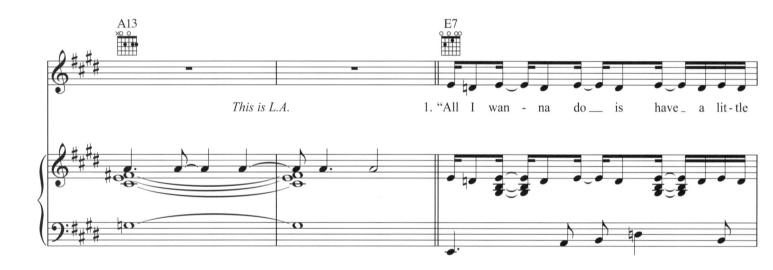

Copyright © 1993 Sony/ATV Music Publishing LLC, Almo Music Corp., Zen Of Iniquity, WC Music Corp., Canvas Mattress Music, Reservoir 416 and Ignorant Music
All Rights on behalf of Sony/ATV Music Publishing LLC Administered by Sony/ATV Music Publishing LLC, 424 Church Street, Suite 1200, Nashville, TN 37219
All Rights on behalf of Zen Of Iniquity Administered by Almo Music Corp.
All Rights on behalf of Canvas Mattress Music Administered by WC Music Corp.
All Rights on behalf of Reservoir 416 Administered by Reservoir Media Management, Inc.
All Rights on behalf of Ignorant Music Administered by Downtown DLJ Songs
International Copyright Secured   All Rights Reserved

ap - ro - pos of noth - ing he says his name is Wil - liam, but I'm

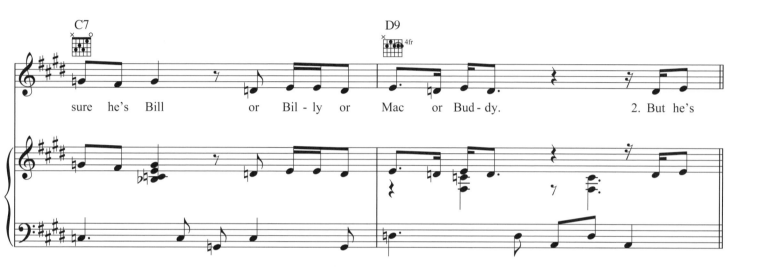

sure he's Bill or Bil - ly or Mac or Bud - dy. 2. But he's

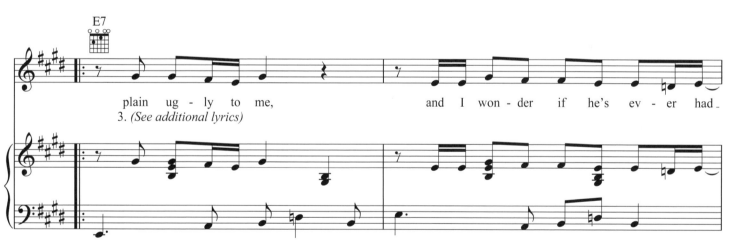

plain ug - ly to me,
3. *(See additional lyrics)*
and I won - der if he's ev - er had

___ a day of fun in his ___ whole life. ___
We are drink - ing beer at

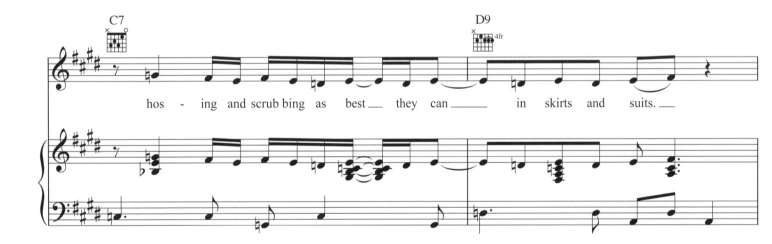

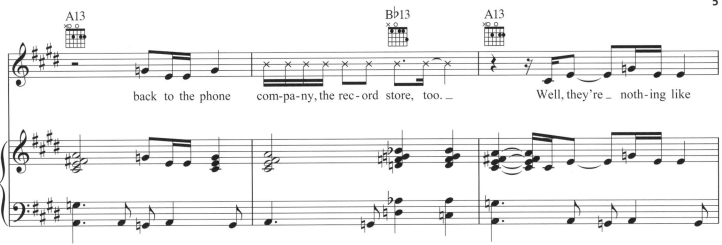

back to the phone com-pa-ny, the rec-ord store, too. _ Well, they're _ noth-ing like

Chorus

Bil-ly and me. _ 'Cause all I wan-na do is have some fun. ___ I got a feel-

-ing I'm not the on - ly one. All I wan-na do is have some fun, _

___ I got a feel - ing I'm not the on - ly one. All I wan-na

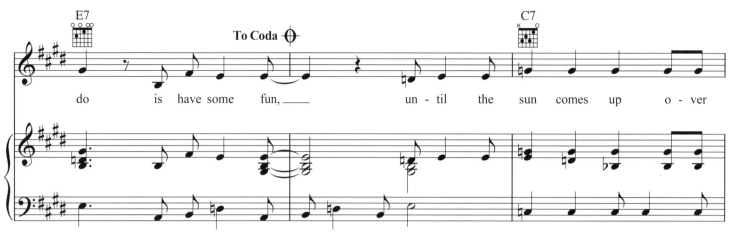

do   is   have   some   fun, ____   un - til   the   sun   comes   up   o - ver

San - ta   Mon - i - ca   Bou - le - vard. ____

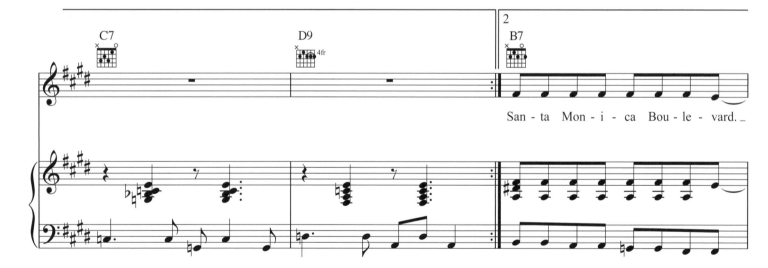

San - ta   Mon - i - ca   Bou - le - vard. ____

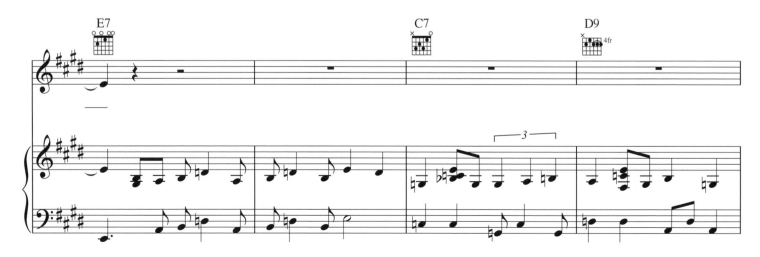

Oth-er - wise __ the bar __ is ours, and the day and the night and the

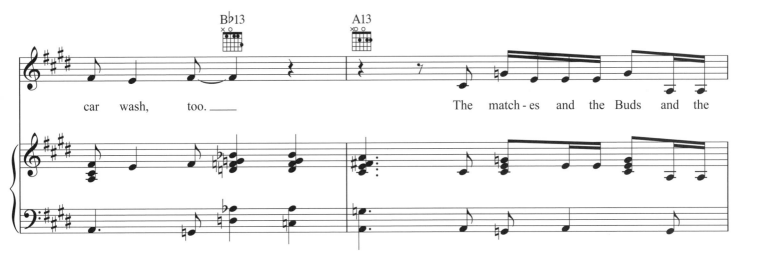

car wash, too. __ The match - es and the Buds and the

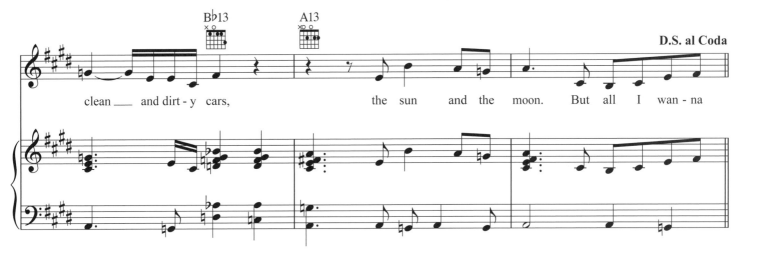

D.S. al Coda

clean __ and dirt - y cars, the sun and the moon. But all I wan - na

un - til the sun comes up o - ver San - ta Mon - i - ca Bou - le - vard. __

__ *(Vocal 1st time only)*

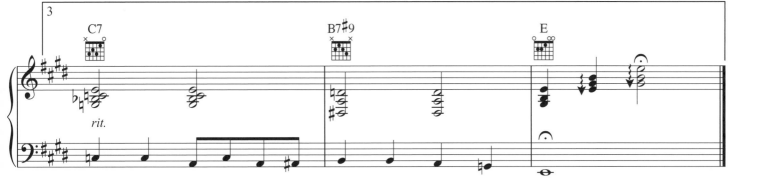

rit.

Additional Lyrics

3. I like a good beer buzz early in the morning,
   And Billy likes to peel the labels from his bottles of Bud
   And shred them on the bar.
   Then he lights every match in an oversized pack,
   Letting each one burn down to his thick fingers
   Before blowing and cursing them out.
   And he's watching the Buds as they spin on the floor.
   A happy couple enters the bar dancing dangerously close to one another.
   The bartender looks up from his want ads.
   Chorus

SOAK UP THE SUN

Words and Music by JEFF TROTT
and SHERYL CROW

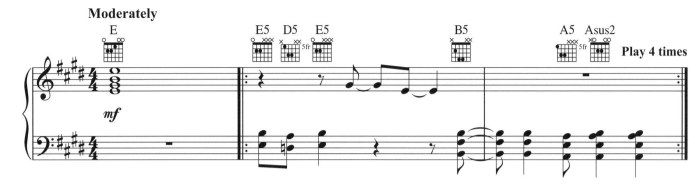

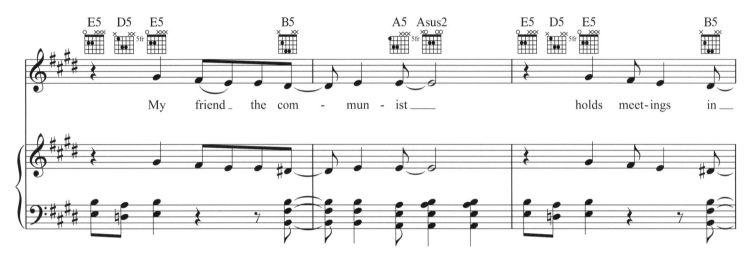

My friend the com - mun - ist ___ holds meet-ings in ___

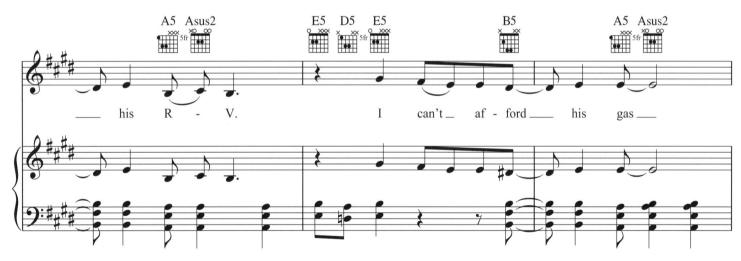

___ his R - V. I can't ___ af - ford ___ his gas ___

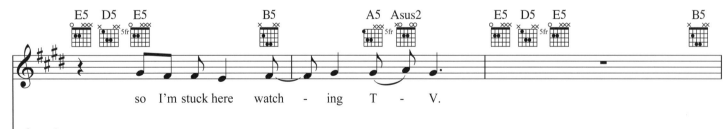

so I'm stuck here watch - ing T - V.

Copyright © 2001 by ole Red Cape Songs, Trottsky Music and Reservoir 416
All Rights for ole Red Cape Songs and Trottsky Music Administered by Anthem Entertainment
All Rights for Reservoir 416 Administered Worldwide by Reservoir Media Management, Inc.
All Rights Reserved   Used by Permission

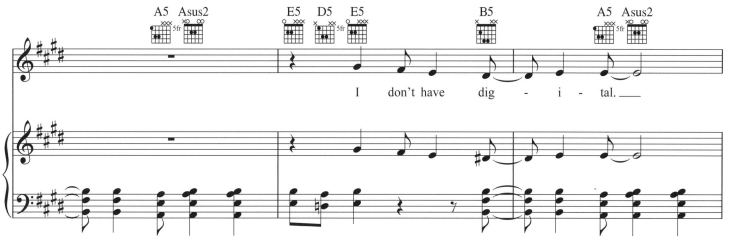

I don't have dig - i - tal. ___

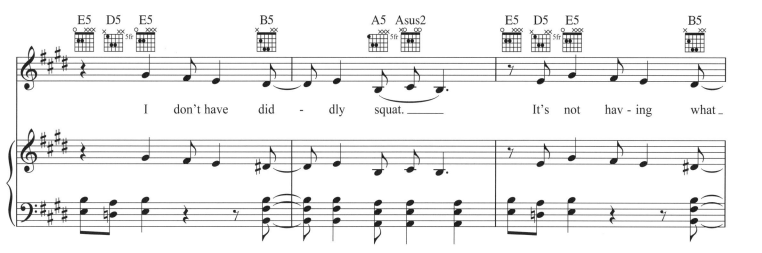

I don't have did - dly squat. ___ It's not hav - ing what ___

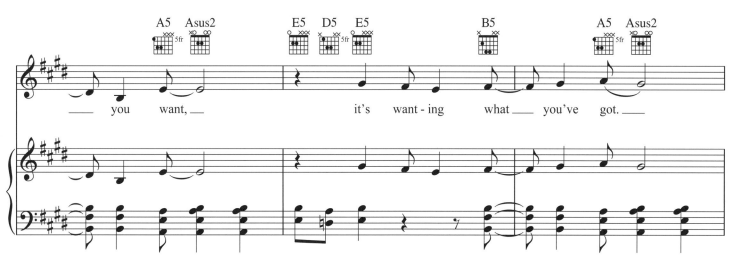

___ you want, ___ it's want - ing what ___ you've got. ___

I'm ___ gon - na soak up the sun. ___

I'm gon - na tell ev -'ry - one ____ to light - en ____ up. ____ I'm gon - na tell 'em that I've ____ ____ got no one to blame. ____ But ev -'ry time I feel lame I'm look - in' ____ up. ____

To Coda ⊕

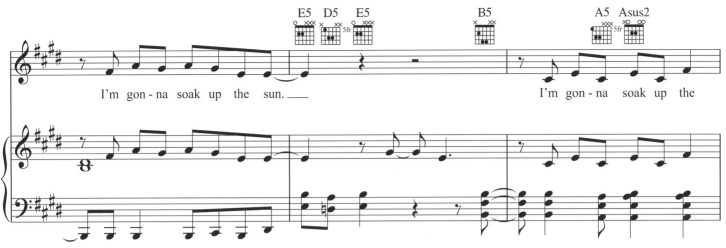

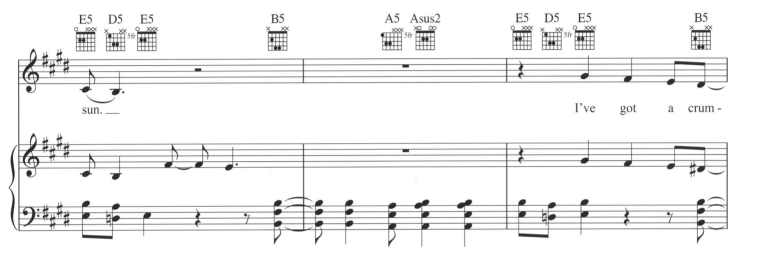

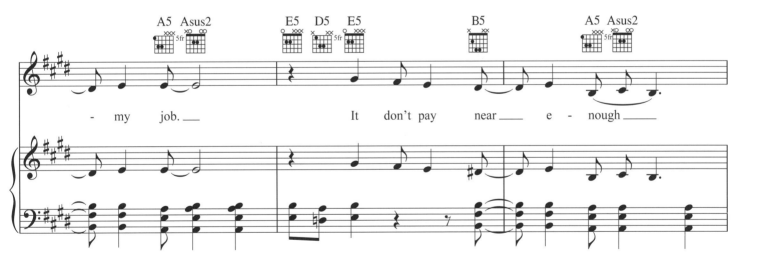

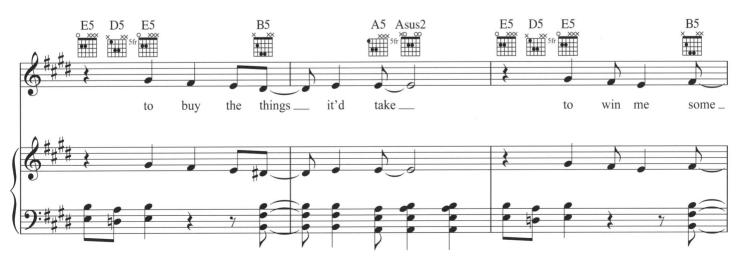

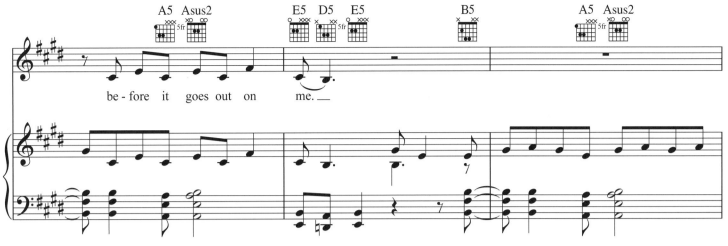

be - fore it goes out on me.

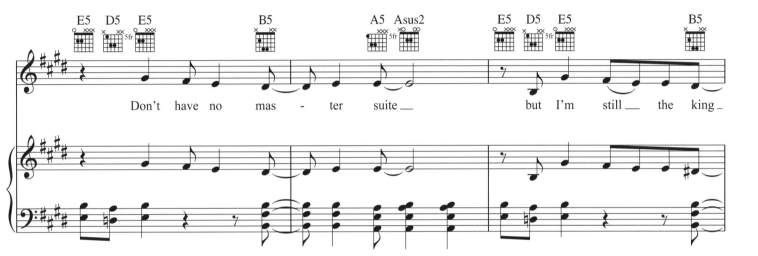

Don't have no mas - ter suite __ but I'm still __ the king __

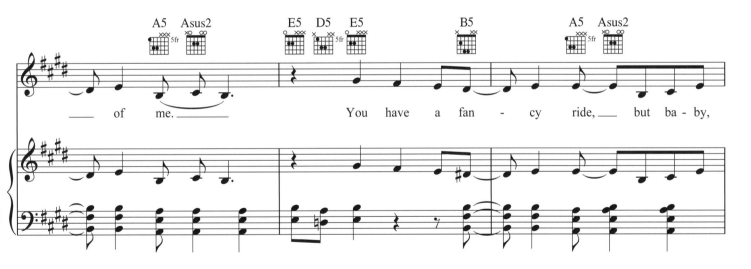

__ of me. __ You have a fan - cy ride, __ but ba - by,

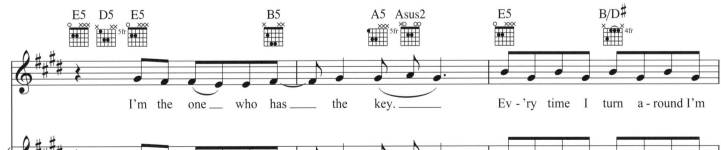

I'm the one __ who has __ the key. __ Ev - 'ry time I turn a - round I'm

I've _____ got no one to blame. _____ But ev-'ry time I feel

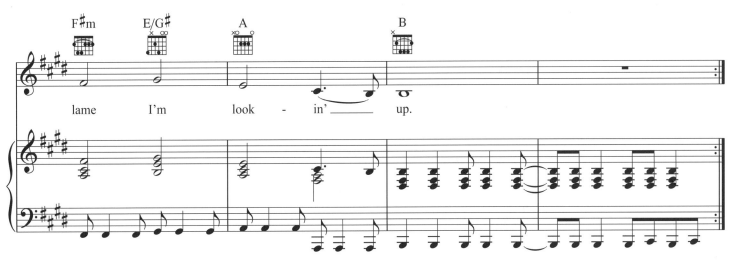

lame I'm look - in' _____ up.

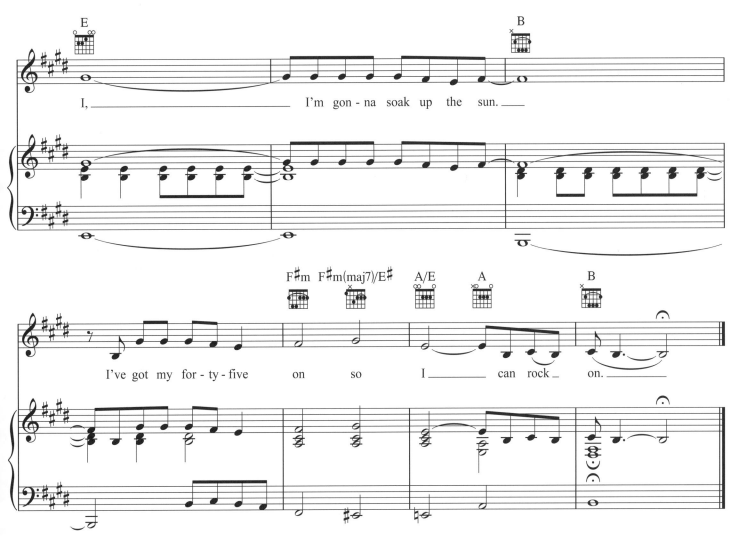

I, _____ I'm gon - na soak up the sun. _____

I've got my for - ty - five on so I _____ can rock _____ on.

MY FAVORITE MISTAKE

Words and Music by SHERYL CROW
and JEFF TROTT

Moderately

I woke up and called __ this morn-ing; the tone of your voice __
Well, your friends act sor - ry for __ me; they watch you pre - tend

__ was a warn - ing that you don't __ care __ for me __ an - y - more. __
__ to a - dore __ me. But I'm no __ fool __ to this game __

Copyright © 1998 Reservoir 416, ole Red Cape Songs and Trottsky Music
All Rights for Reservoir 416 Administered by Reservoir Media Management, Inc.
All Rights for ole Red Cape Songs and Trottsky Music Administered by Anthem Entertainment
All Rights Reserved   Used by Permission

I made up the bed __
Now here comes your se -

__ we sleep __ in;
-cret lov - er;

I looked at the clock __ when you creep __ in.
she'll be un - like an - y __ oth - er

It's six A. M. __ and I'm __ a - lone. __
un - til your guilt __ goes up __ in flames. __

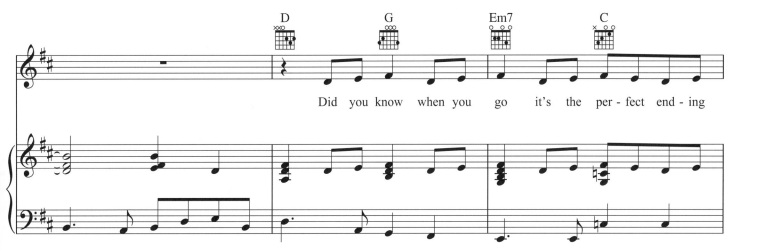

Did you know when you go it's the per - fect end - ing

to the bad day   I was just be - gin - ning?   When you go,   all   I

know   is you're my   fa - v'rite mis - take. _____

_____   You're my   fa - v'rite mis - take. _____

Well, may-be noth - ing lasts ___ for - ev - er, e -

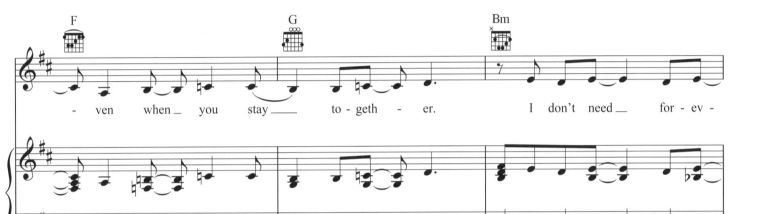

- ven when ___ you stay ___ to - geth - er. I don't need ___ for - ev -

- er af - ter, but it's your laugh - ter, won't ___ let me go; ___ so I'm hold -

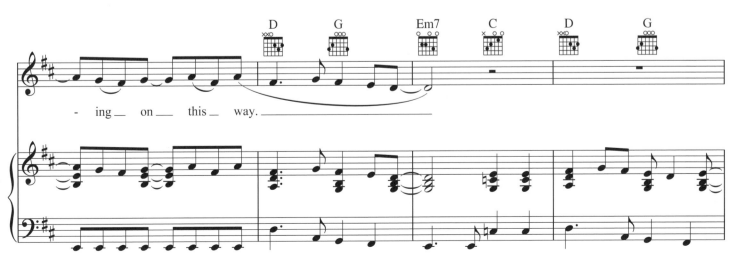

- ing ___ on ___ this ___ way. _____

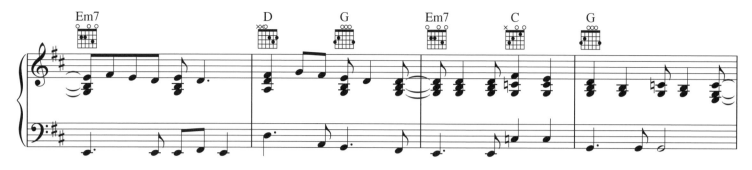

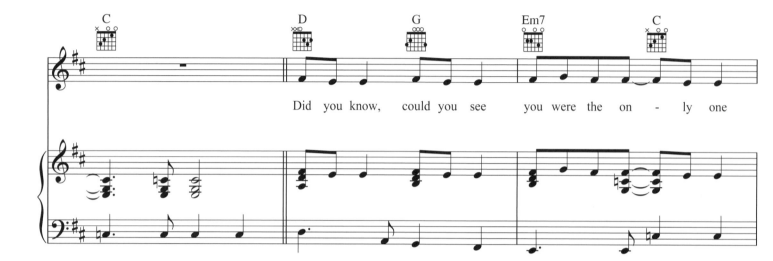

Did you know, could you see you were the on - ly one

that I ev - er loved? __ Now ev - 'ry - thing's so wrong.

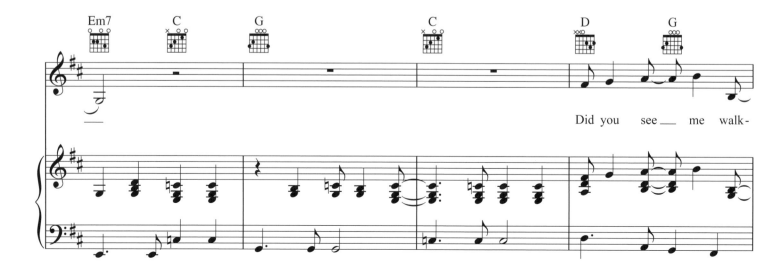

Did you see __ me walk-

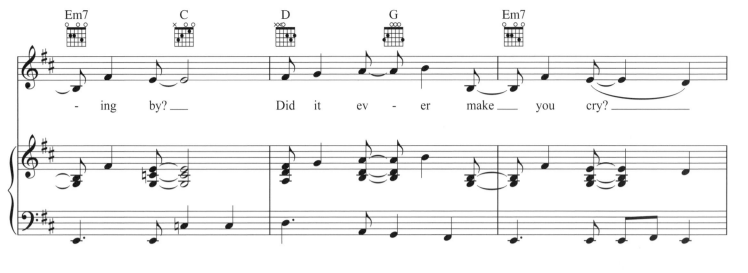

-ing by? ___ Did it ev - er make ___ you cry? ___

Now you're my fa - 'rite mis - take. ___

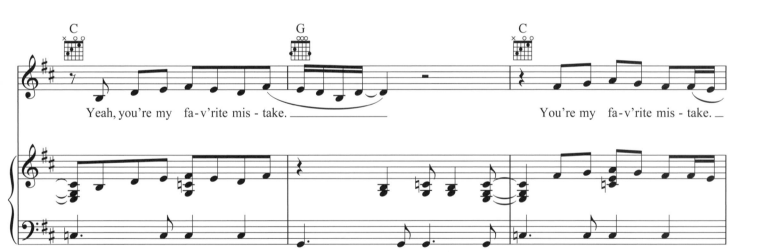

Yeah, you're my fa - v'rite mis - take. ___   You're my fa - v'rite mis - take. _

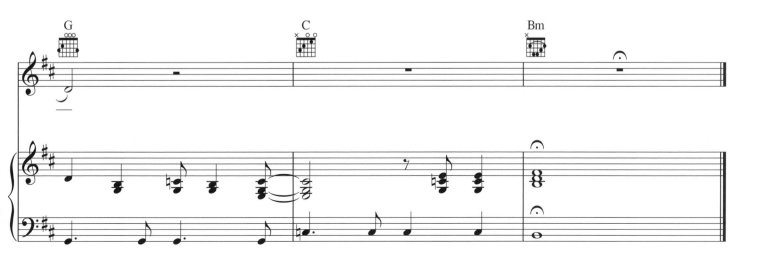

THE FIRST CUT IS THE DEEPEST

Words and Music by
CAT STEVENS

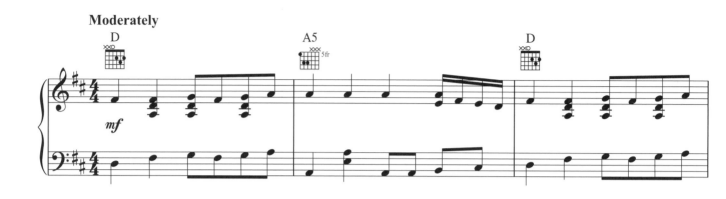

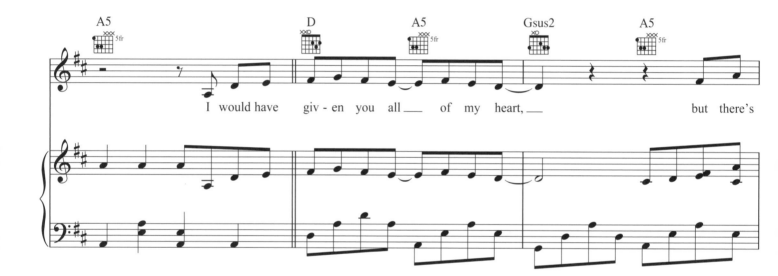

I would have giv-en you all __ of my heart, __ but there's

some-one who's torn it a-part __ and he's tak-en just all __ that I had. __

Copyright © 1967 SALAFA LTD.
Copyright Renewed
All Rights in the U.S. and Canada Controlled and Administered by UNIVERSAL MUSIC CORP.
All Rights Reserved   Used by Permission

I still want you by my side

just to help me dry the tears that I've cried. And I'm

sure gon-na give you a try. If you want, I'll try to love a-gain, try.

Ba-by, I'll try to love a-gain, but I know, oh,

the first cut is the deep - est. Ba - by, I know __ the first cut is the deep-

- est. And when it comes to be - ing luck - y, he's cursed. __ And when it

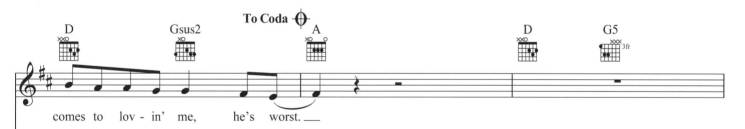

comes to lov - in' me, he's worst. __

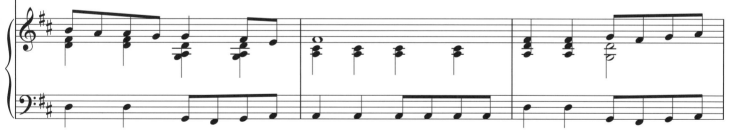

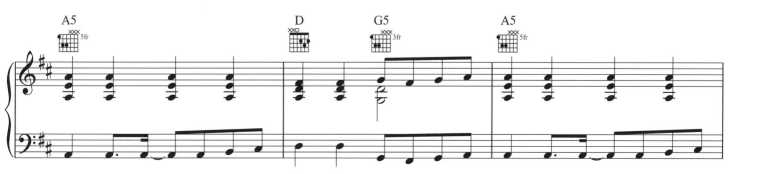

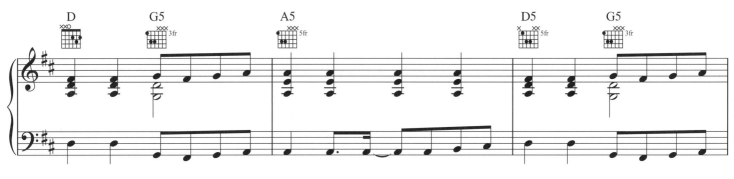

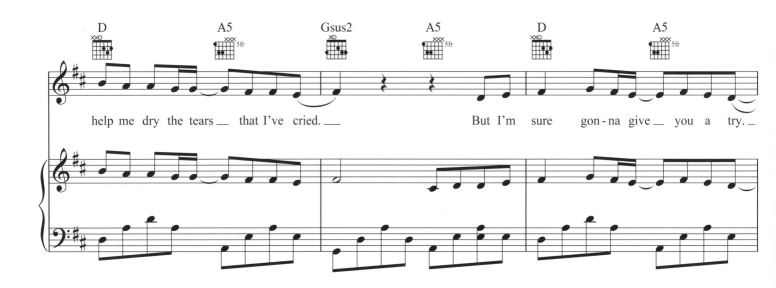

I still want___ you by___ my___ side _____ just to
help me dry the tears___ that I've cried. ___ But I'm sure gon-na give___ you a try. ___

_____ 'Cause if you want, I'll try to love a - gain, try to love a - gain,

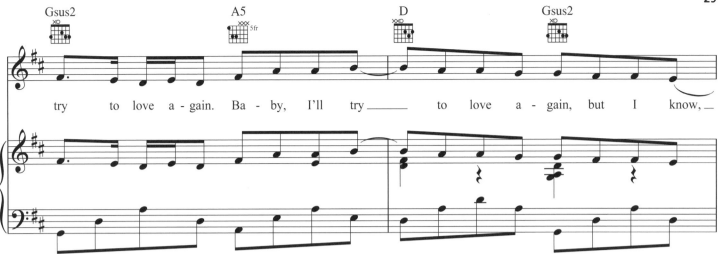

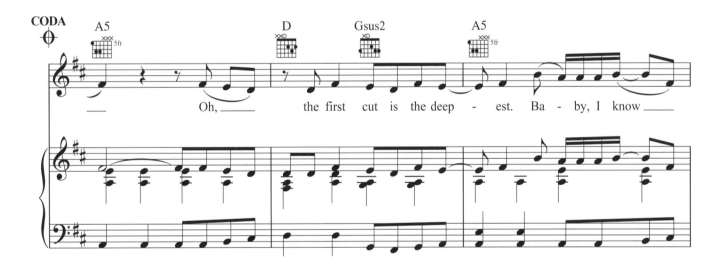

EVERYDAY IS A WINDING ROAD

Words and Music by JEFF TROTT,
SHERYL CROW and BRIAN McLEOD

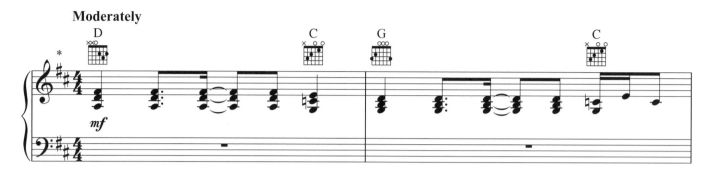

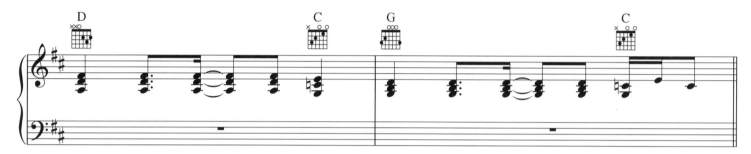

I hitched a ride ___ with a vend - ing ma - chine re - pair - man.
He's got a daugh - ter he calls Eas - ter,

He says he's been ___ down that road more than twice. ___ He ___ was high on
she was born ___ on a Tues - day night. ___ I'm ___ just won - d'ring

Recorded a half step lower.

Copyright © 1996, 2001 by ole Red Cape Songs, Trottsky Music, Reservoir 416, Warner-Tamerlane Publishing Corp. and Weenie Stand Music
All Rights for ole Red Cape Songs and Trottsky Music Administered by Anthem Entertainment
All Rights for Reservoir 416 Administered by Reservoir Media Management, Inc.
All Rights for Weenie Stand Music Administered by Warner-Tamerlane Publishing Corp.
All Rights Reserved   Used by Permission

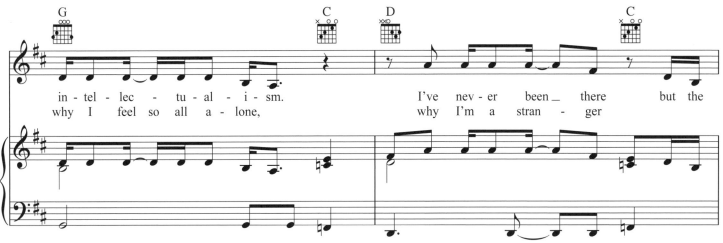

in - tel - lec - tu - al - i - sm. I've nev - er been __ there but the
why I feel so all a - lone, why I'm a stran - ger

bro - chure __ looks nice.) Jump in, ___ let's go. ___
in my ___ own life.)

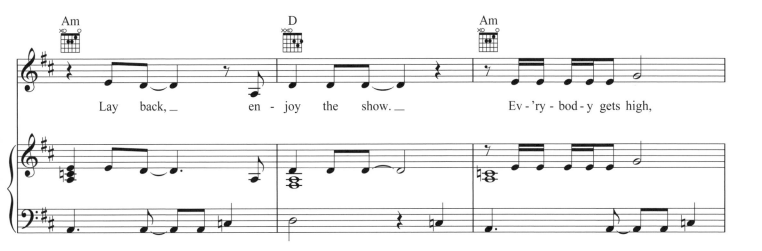

Lay back, __ en - joy the show. __ Ev - 'ry - bod - y gets high,

ev - 'ry - bod - y gets low. These are the days __ when an - y - thing goes. __ Ev - 'ry-

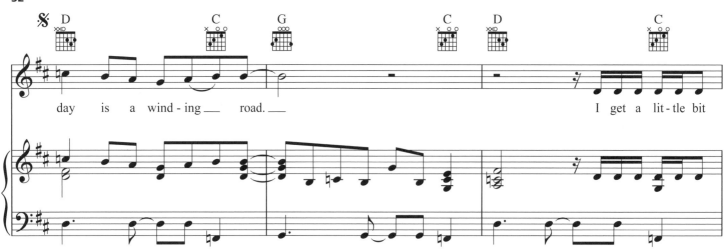

day is a wind-ing road. I get a lit-tle bit

clos-er. Ev-'ry-day is a fad-ed sign.

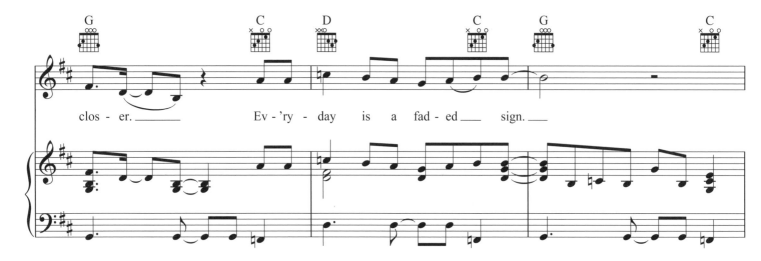

I get a lit-tle bit clos-er to feel-ing fine.

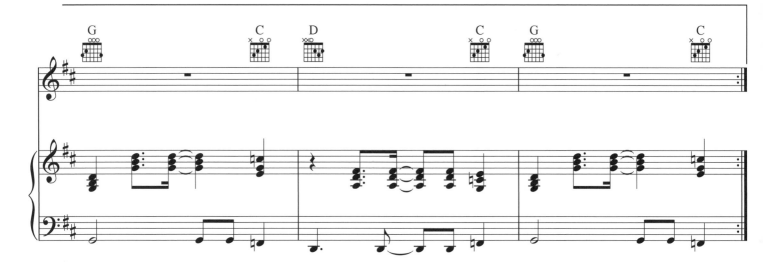

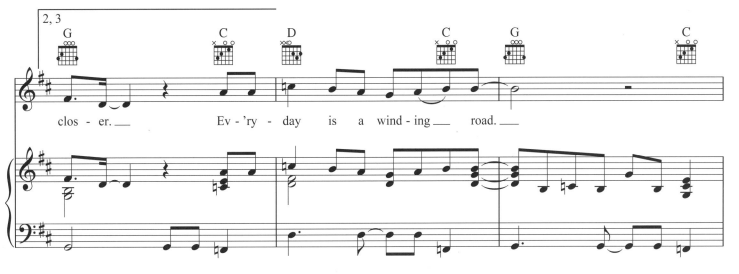

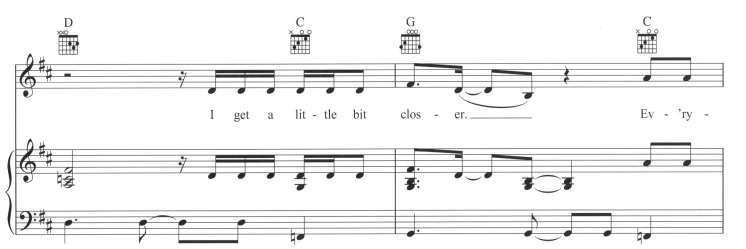

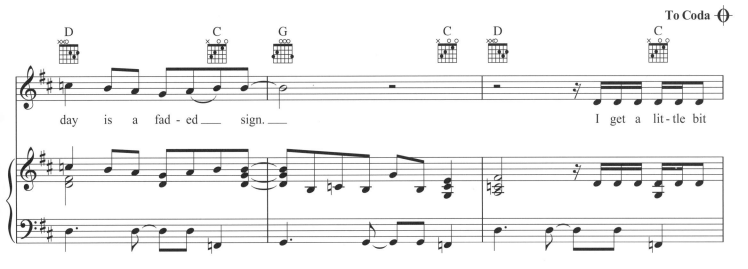

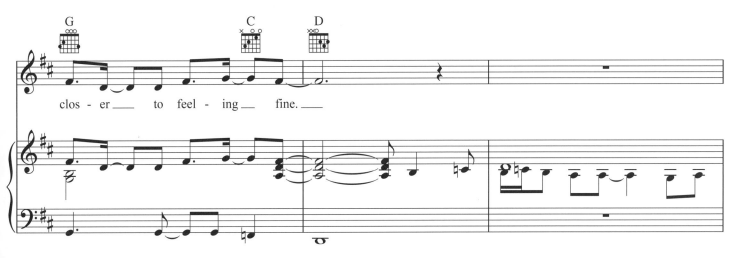

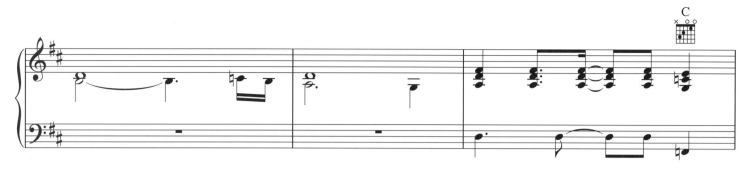

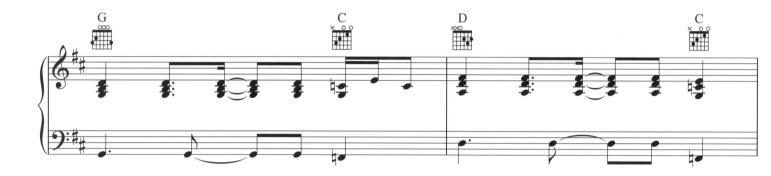

I've been swim-ming in a

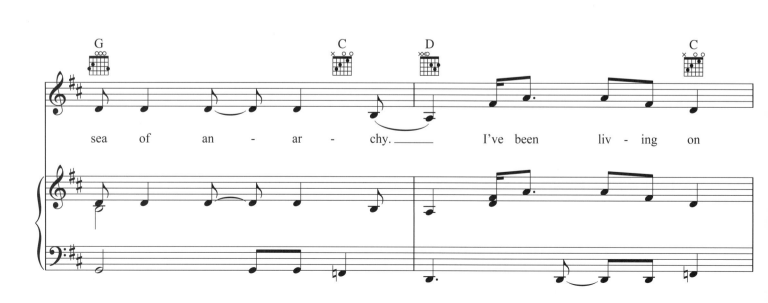

sea of an - ar - chy._____ I've been liv - ing on

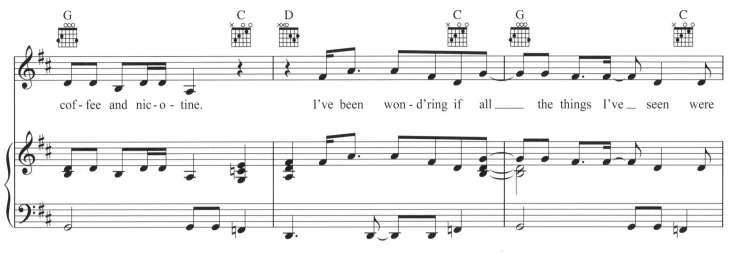

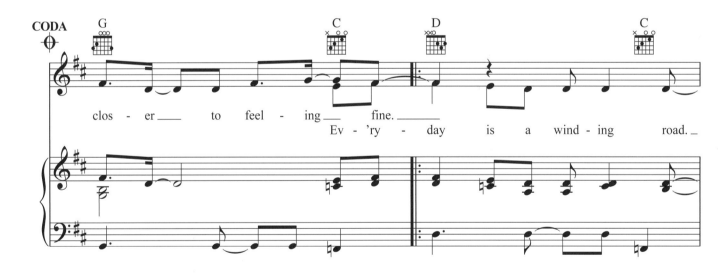

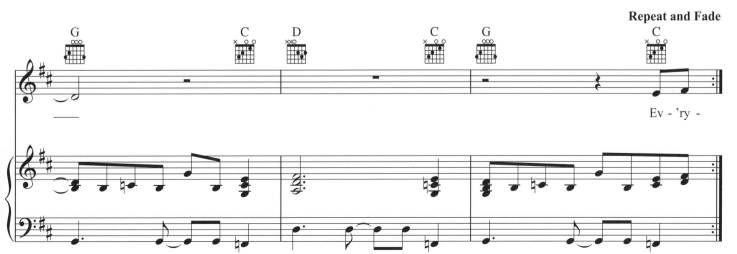

LEAVING LAS VEGAS

Words and Music by SHERYL CROW,
DAVID RICKETTS, KEVIN GILBERT,
BILL BOTTRELL and DAVID BAERWALD

Moderately

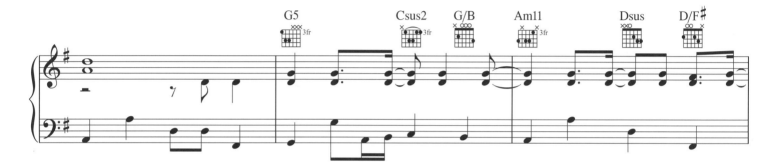

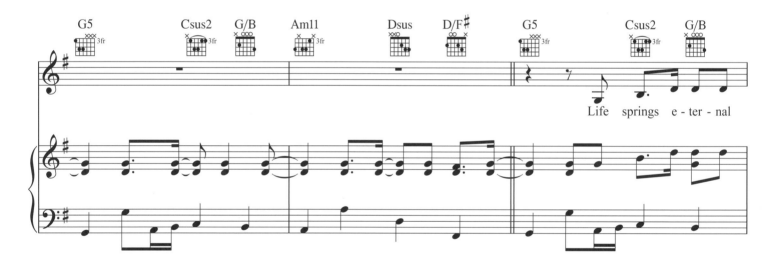

Life springs e-ter-nal

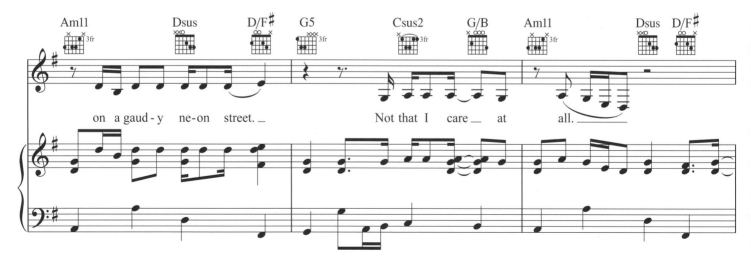

on a gaud-y ne-on street. ___ Not that I care ___ at all.

Copyright © 1993, 1994 Reservoir 416, Sony/ATV Music Publishing LLC, 48/11 Music, Ignorant Music, Almo Music Corp. and Zen Of Iniquity
All Rights for Reservoir 416 Administered Worldwide by Reservoir Media Management, Inc.
All Rights for Sony/ATV Music Publishing LLC and 48/11 Music Administered by Sony/ATV Music Publishing LLC, 424 Church Street, Suite 1200, Nashville, TN 37219
All Rights for Ignorant Music Administered by Downtown DLJ Songs
All Rights for Zen Of Iniquity Administered by Almo Music Corp.
All Rights Reserved   Used by Permission

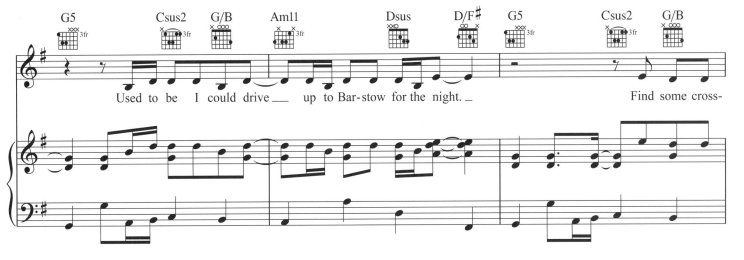

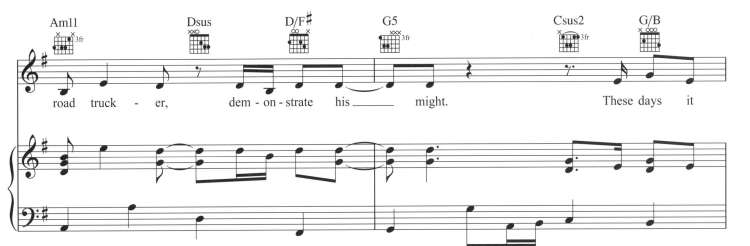

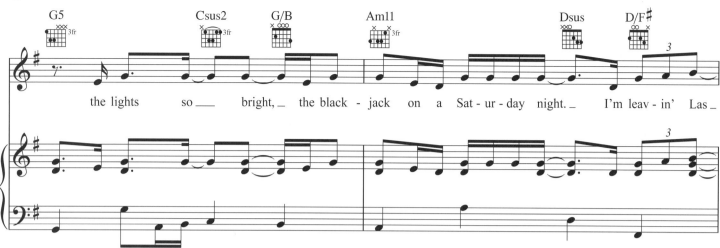

the lights so ___ bright, ___ the black-jack on a Sat-ur-day night. ___ I'm leav-in' Las ___

___ Ve-gas. _____ I'm leav-in' for ___ good. I'm leav-in' for ___

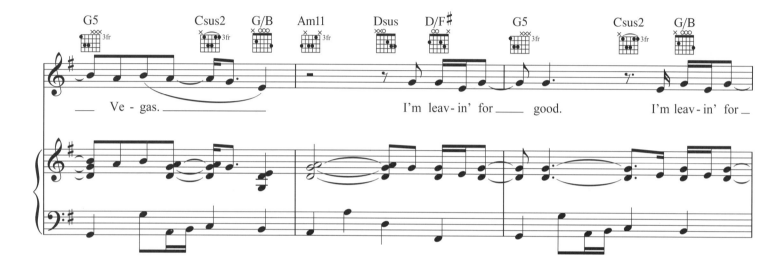

___ good, for good. ___ I'm stand-in' in the mid-dle of the des-ert wait-in' for my

ship to come ___ in. _____ But now no jok-er,

no jack, no king   can take this los-in' hand — and,   and make it win. — I'm leav-in' Las

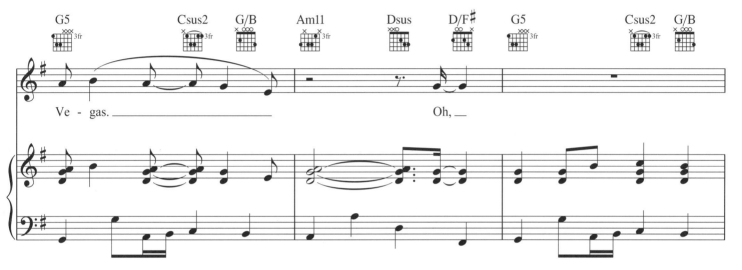

Ve - gas. _____   Oh, __

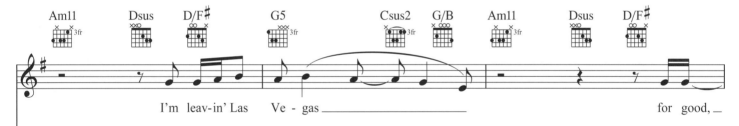

I'm leav-in' Las   Ve - gas _____   for good, __

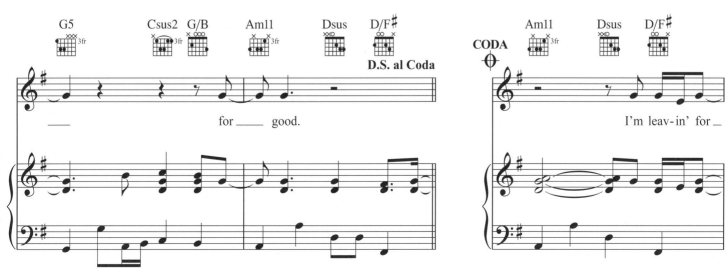

__   for ___ good.   I'm leav-in' for __

D.S. al Coda

CODA

LIGHT IN YOUR EYES

Words and Music by SHERYL CROW
and JOHN SHANKS

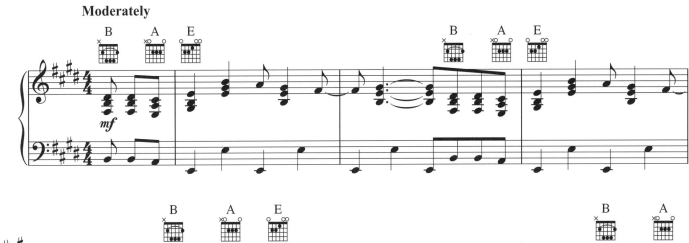

Some-thing is happ - n'in'.
No use pre - tend - in'.

Ev - 'ry-thing's dif - f'rent but ev - 'ry-thing is fine, _____ yeah. _
You nev - er ex - ist - ed un - til you saw the light, _____ yeah. _

And this is the good _____ stuff.
And you're just be - gin - ning.

Copyright © 2003 Reservoir 416 and Sony/ATV Music Publishing LLC
All Rights for Reservoir 416 Administered Worldwide by Reservoir Media Management, Inc.
All Rights for Sony/ATV Music Publishing LLC Administered by Sony/ATV Music Publishing LLC, 424 Church Street, Suite 1200, Nashville, TN 37219
All Rights Reserved   Used by Permission

And yes-ter-day's on - ly ___ what you leave be - hind. ___
You ___ hav-en't missed ___ it, it's all a-head of you ___

It's on - ly in your mind. ___
and you know what to do. ___

You got - ta
You got - ta

(1., 2.) talk to the one who made ___ you. ___
(D.S.) talk to the one who loves ___ you. ___

Talk to the one who un - der - stands. ___

Talk to the one who gave ___ you ___ all the ___ light in your eyes. ___ All the

light in your eyes. ___ Here comes the world ___ and she ___ is

beau - ti - f'ly mys - te - ri - ous. She's got it all ___ and you ___ say,

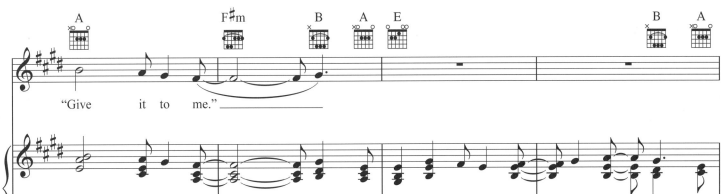

"Give it to me." _____

No-bod-y's hap - py. That's not the world ___ I ___ knew in-side ___

___ where ev-'ry-bod-y hides. ___ You got-ta

talk to the one who made ___ you. ___ Talk to the one who un - der - stands. ___

Talk to the one who gave ___ you all the ___ light in your eyes. ___ You got-ta

Yeah, _____ thank _ you, thank _ you.

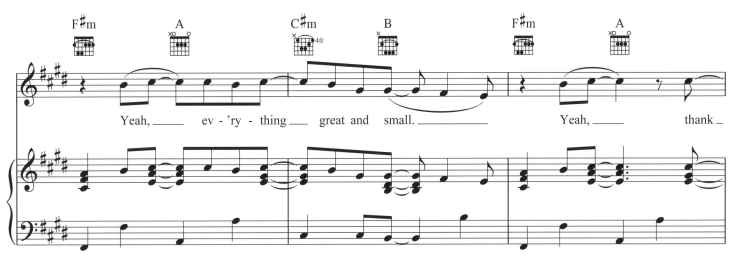

Yeah, _____ ev - 'ry - thing _ great and small. _____ Yeah, _____ thank _

_ you, thank _ you for the light in your eyes. _____

For the light in your eyes. _____

STRONG ENOUGH

Words and Music by KEVIN GILBERT,
DAVID BAERWALD, SHERYL CROW,
BRIAN McLEOD, BILL BOTTRELL
and DAVID RICKETTS

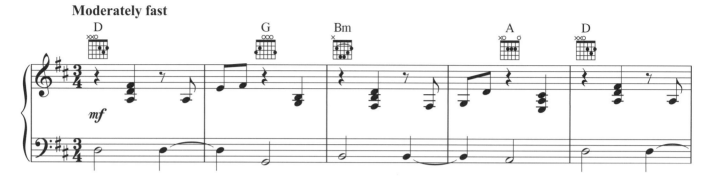

Copyright © 1993, 1994, 1999 Sony/ATV Music Publishing LLC, 48/11 Music, Almo Music Corp., Reservoir 416,
Warner-Tamerlane Publishing Corp., Third Stone From The Sun Music, Weenie Stand Music and Ignorant Music
All Rights on behalf of Sony/ATV Music Publishing LLC and 48/11 Music Administered by Sony/ATV Music Publishing LLC, 424 Church Street, Suite 1200, Nashville, TN 37219
All Rights on behalf of Reservoir 416 Administered Worldwide by Reservoir Media Management, Inc.
All Rights on behalf of Third Stone From The Sun Music and Weenie Stand Music Administered by Warner-Tamerlane Publishing Corp.
All Rights on behalf of Ignorant Music Administered by Downtown DLJ Songs
International Copyright Secured   All Rights Reserved

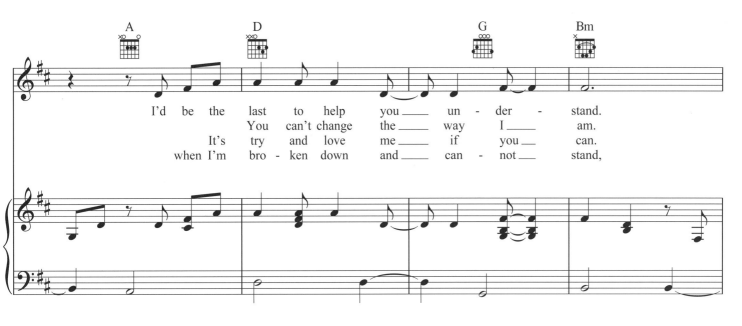

I'd be the last to help you _____ un - der - stand.
You can't change the _____ way I _____ am.
It's try and love me _____ if you _____ can.
when I'm bro - ken down and _____ can - not _____ stand,

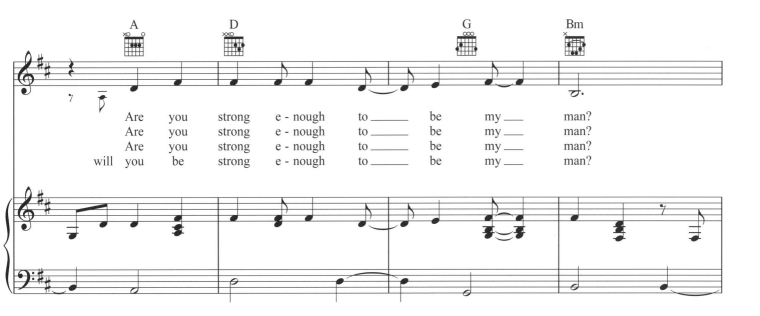

Are you strong e - nough to _____ be my _____ man?
Are you strong e - nough to _____ be my _____ man?
Are you strong e - nough to _____ be my _____ man?
will you be strong e - nough to _____ be my _____ man?

1, 3

My _____ man.
My _____ man.

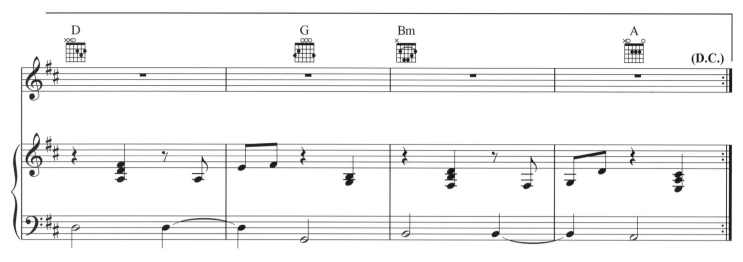

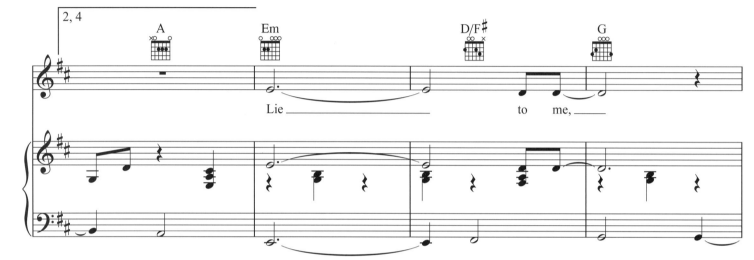

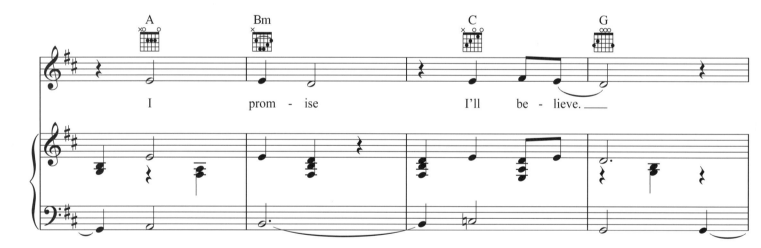

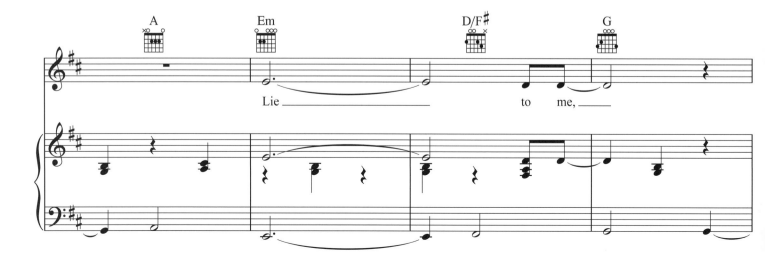

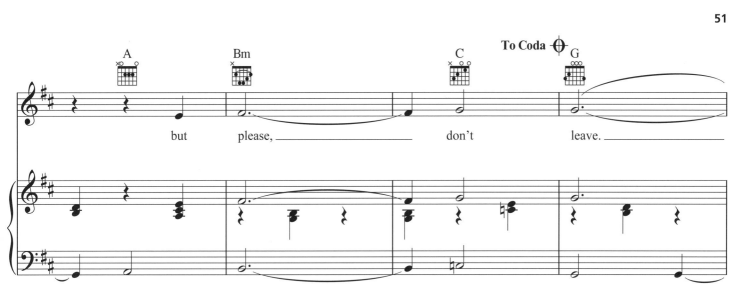

but please, _____ don't leave. _____

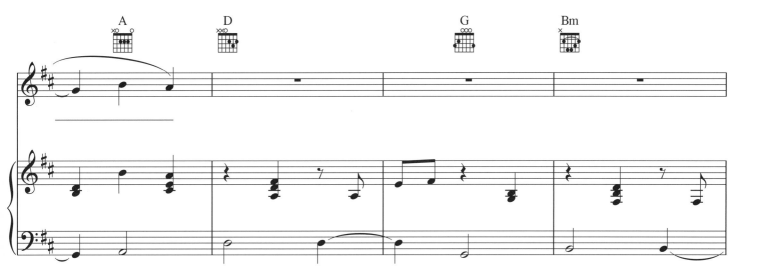

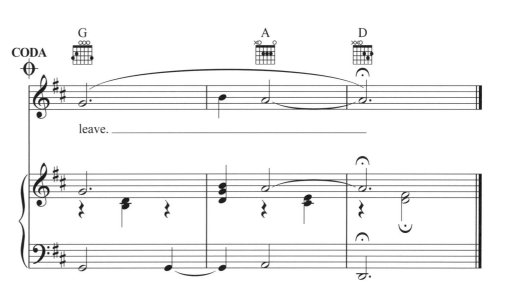

leave. _____

IF IT MAKES YOU HAPPY

Words and Music by JEFF TROTT
and SHERYL CROW

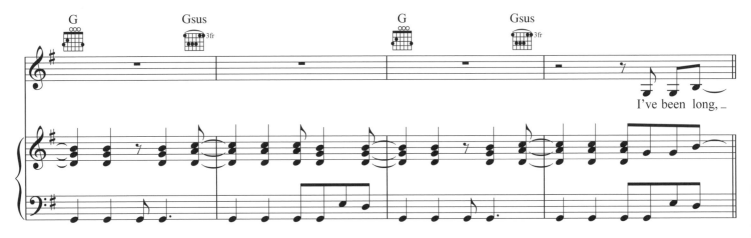

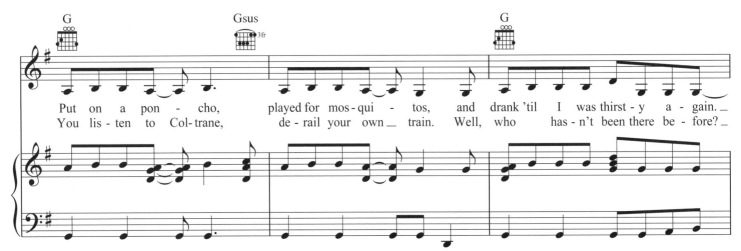

Copyright © 1996, 2001 Reservoir 416, ole Red Cape Songs and Trottsky Music
All Rights for Reservoir 416 Administered Worldwide by Reservoir Media Management, Inc.
All Rights for ole Red Cape Songs and Trottsky Music Administered by Anthem Entertainment
All Rights Reserved   Used by Permission

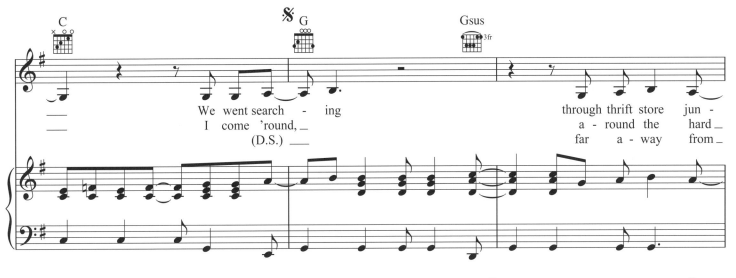

We went search - ing
I come 'round, __
(D.S.) __

through thrift store jun -
a - round the hard
far a - way from __

- gles,
__ way.
__ here.

found Ge - ron - i - mo's ri - fle,
Bring you com - ics in bed, __ scrape the
Put on a pon - cho,

Mar - i - lyn's sham - poo and
mold off the bread, __ and
played for mos - qui - tos, and

Ben - ny Good - man's cor - set and pen. __
serve you French toast a - gain. __
ev - 'ry - where in be - tween. __

Well, o - kay, __
Well, o - kay, __
Well, o - kay, __

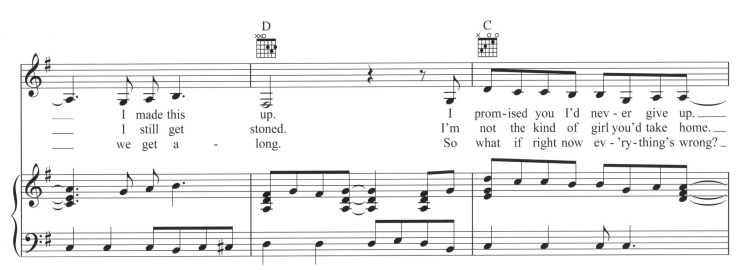

I made this up.
I still get stoned.
we get a - long.

I prom - ised you I'd nev - er give up. __
I'm not the kind of girl you'd take home. __
So what if right now ev - 'ry - thing's wrong? __

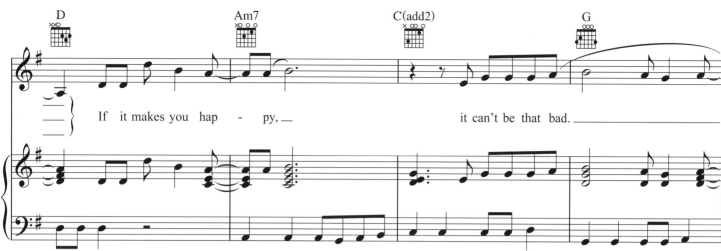

If it makes you hap - py, ___ it can't be that bad. ___

___ If it makes you hap - py, ___ then why the hell are you so ___ sad?

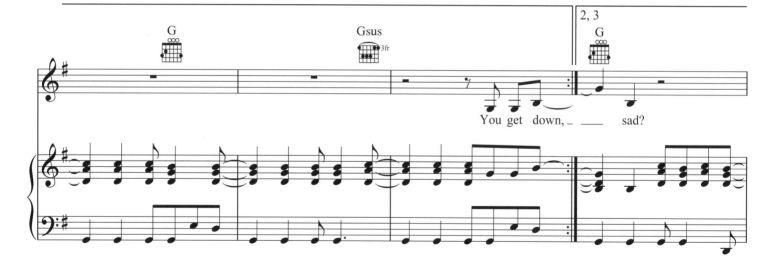

You get down, ___ ___ sad?

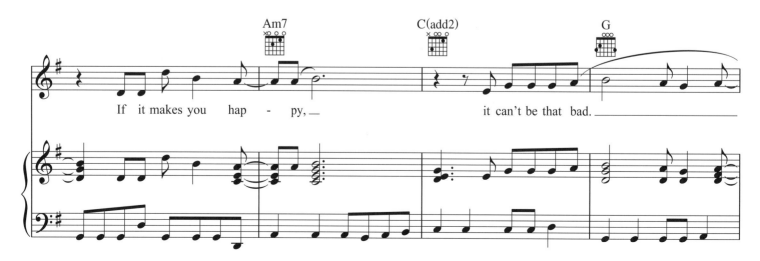

If it makes you hap - py, ___ it can't be that bad. ___

If it makes you hap - py, ___ then why the hell are you so ___ sad?

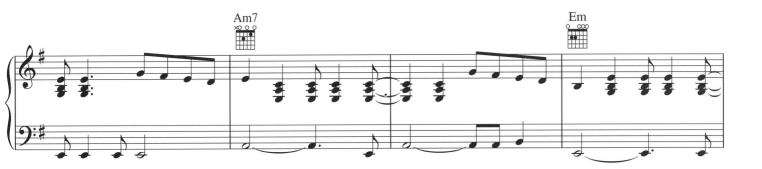

D.S. al Coda
(take 2nd ending)

We've been far, ___

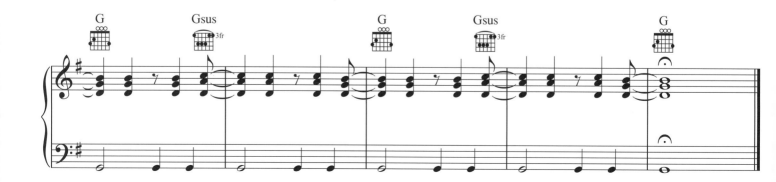

THE DIFFICULT KIND

Words and Music by
SHERYL CROW

Copyright © 1998 Reservoir 416
All Rights Administered worldwide by Reservoir Media Management, Inc.
All Rights Reserved   Used by Permission

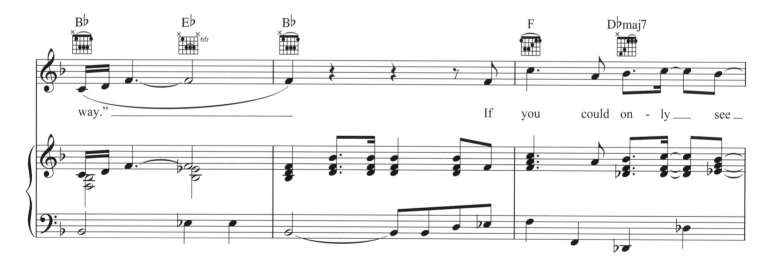

I'd no long-er __ be, __ in your mind, the dif-fi-cult kind. __

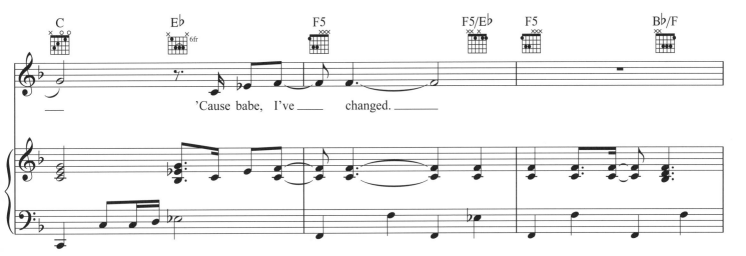

__ 'Cause babe, I've __ changed. __

Tell it to __ me slow, __ tell me with __ your eyes. __
ball - break - in' moon __ and rid - i - cul - ing stars. __

__ If an - y - one __ should know __ how to let __ it
__ Oh, the old - er __ I get, __ the clos - er __ you

slide. _____

are. _____

I swear __ I __ can see __ you _____

Don't __ you __ got some - where _____

__ com-in' up __ the drive. _____

__ that you __ need __ to be? _____

And there ain't

In -

noth-in' like __ re - gret _____ to re-mind you you're __ a-live. _____

stead of hang - ing __ here _____ mak-in' a fool __ of me. _____

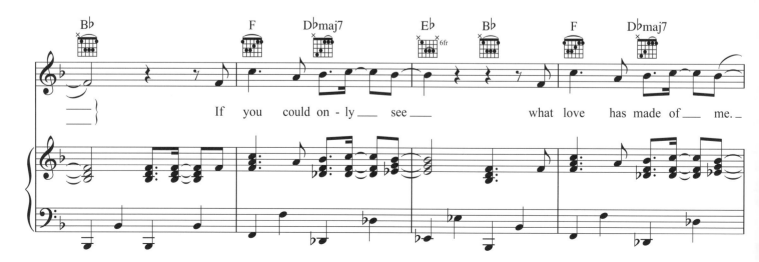

If you could on - ly __ see __ what love has made of __ me. __

Then I'd no long-er ___ be, ___ in your mind, the dif-fi-cult kind. ___

'Cause babe, I've ___ changed. ___ I crossed the can - yon a

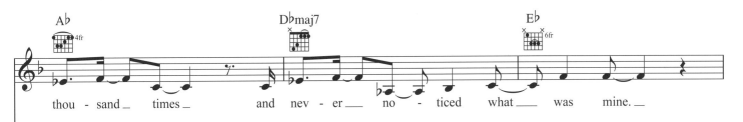

thou - sand ___ times ___ and nev - er ___ no - ticed what ___ was mine. ___

What you'll re-mem - ber of me to - night, ___ well, it al - most ___ makes me cry. ___ Yeah, it

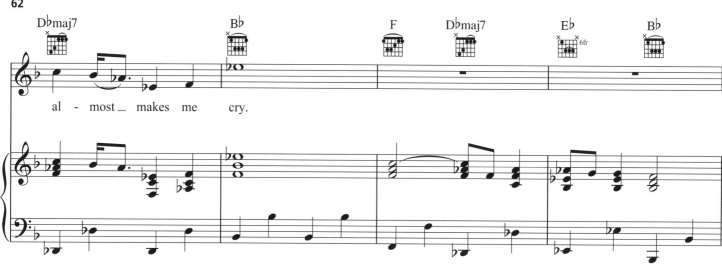

al - most__ makes me cry.

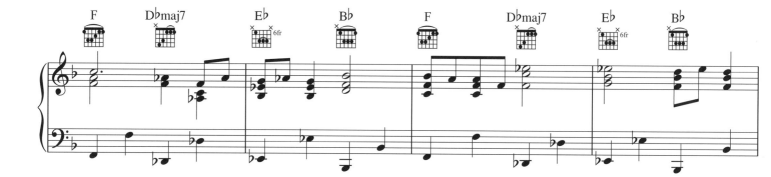

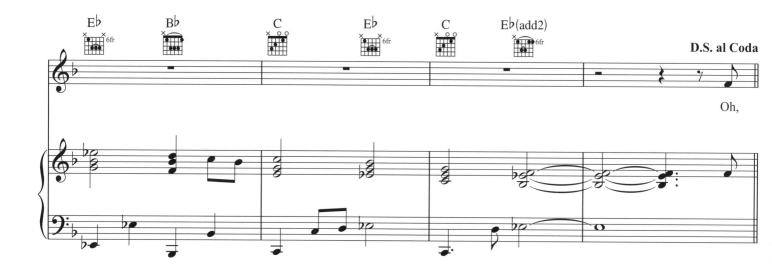

D.S. al Coda

Oh,

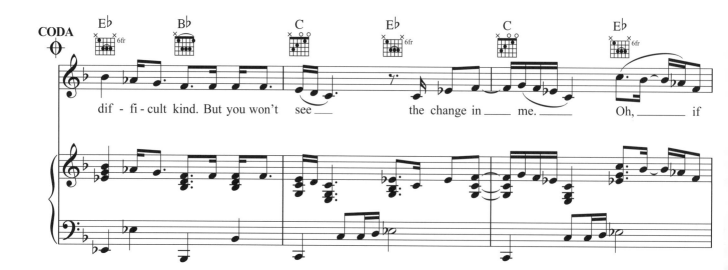

dif - fi - cult kind. But you won't see ___ the change in ___ me. ___ Oh, ___ if

you could on-ly ___ see ____ what love has made of ___ me. ___

But I'll for-ev-er ___ be, ___ in your mind, the dif-fi-cult kind. But you won't ___

___ see. ___ No, you won't ___ see _____ the good in me. _____ But babe, I've ___

___ changed. _____ Yes babe, I've ___ changed. _

PICTURE

Words and Music by R.J. RITCHIE
and SHERYL CROW

1. Liv-in' my life in a slow hell; dif-f'rent
2. called you last night in the ho-tel.
3. *Instrumental solo ad lib.*
4. *(See additional lyrics)*

girl ev-'ry night at the ho-tel. I ain't seen the sun
Ev-'ry-one knows but they won't tell. But their half heart-ed smiles tell me

© 2002 WARNER-TAMERLANE PUBLISHING CORP., THIRTY TWO MILE MUSIC and RESERVOIR 416
All Rights for THIRTY TWO MILE MUSIC Administered by WARNER-TAMERLANE PUBLISHING CORP.
All Rights for RESERVOIR 416 Administered Worldwide by RESERVOIR MEDIA MANAGEMENT, INC.
All Rights Reserved   Used by Permission

pic - ture a - way; _____
pic - ture a - way; _____
pic - ture to - day. _____

sat down and cried ___ to - day. _____
I won - der where ___ you been. _____
I swear I'll change ___ my ways. _____

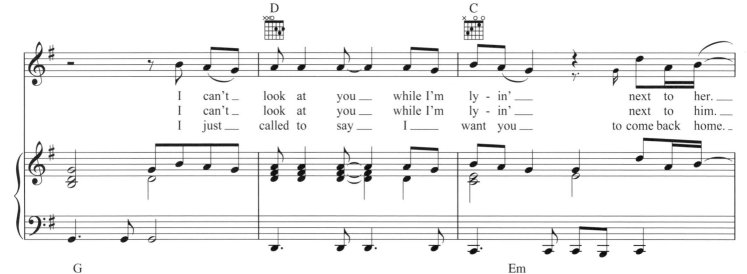

I can't ___ look at you ___ while I'm ly - in' ___ next to her. ___
I can't ___ look at you ___ while I'm ly - in' ___ next to him. ___
I just ___ called to say ___ I ___ want you ___ to come back home. _

_____
_____
_____

I put your pic - ture a - way, _____
I put your pic - ture a - way, _____
I found your pic - ture to - day. _____

sat down and cried ___ to - day. _____
I won - der where ___ you been. _____
I swear I'll change ___ my ways. _____

I can't ___
I can't ___
I just ___

Additional Lyrics

Verse 3: I saw you yesterday with an old friend.
It was the same ol' same "How have you been?"
Since you been gone,
My world's been dark and gray.

Verse 4: You reminded me of brighter days.
I hoped you were comin' home to stay.
I was headed to church; I was off to drink you away.
I thought about you for a long time.
Can't seem to get you off my mind.
I can't understand why we're livin' life this way.

STEVE McQUEEN

Words and Music by SHERYL CROW
and JOHN SHANKS

Copyright © 2002 Reservoir 416 and Sony/ATV Music Publishing LLC
All Rights for Reservoir 416 Administered Worldwide by Reservoir Media Management, Inc.
All Rights for Sony/ATV Music Publishing LLC Administered by Sony/ATV Music Publishing LLC, 424 Church Street, Suite 1200, Nashville, TN 37219
All Rights Reserved   Used by Permission

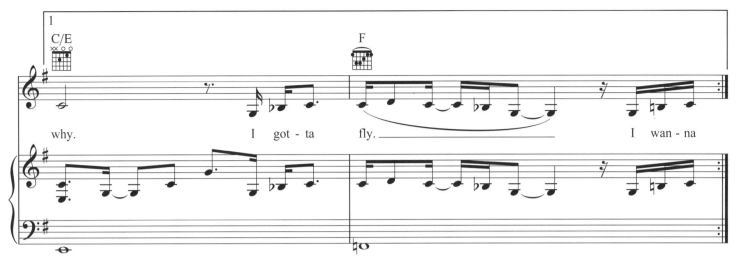

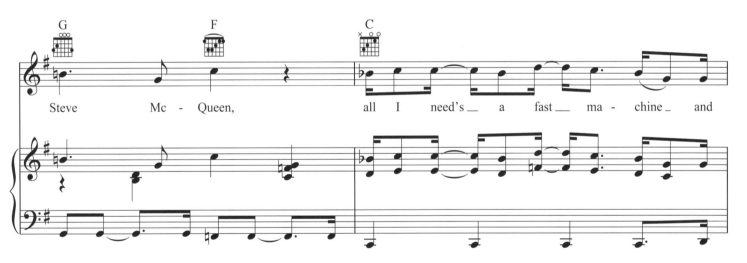

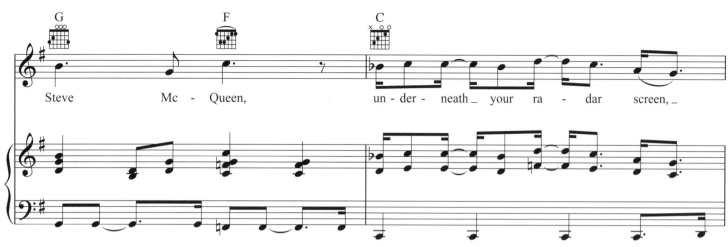

Steve Mc - Queen, un - der - neath your ra - dar screen, _

you'll nev - er catch ___ me to - night. ___

Like Steve Mc - Queen,

like Steve Mc - Queen,

We got rock stars in the White __ House, and all our

pop stars look like porn. __ All my he-roes hit the high - way, 'cause they don't

hang out here __ no more. __ Well, you can call me on __ my cell __ phone, you can

page me all __ night long. __ But you won't catch __ this free - bird, I'll al -

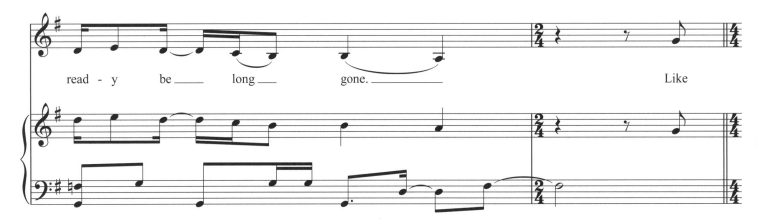

read - y be ___ long ___ gone. ___

Like

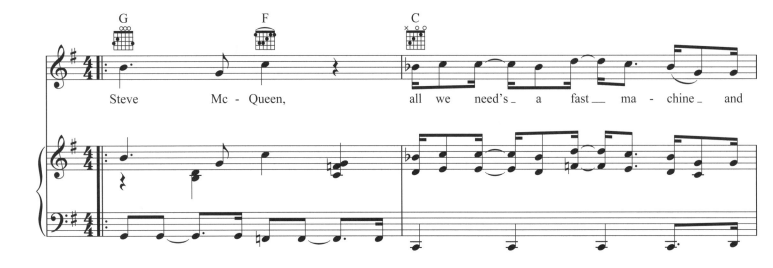

Steve Mc - Queen, all we need's a fast ___ ma - chine ___ and

we're gon - na make ___ it all ___ right ___ like

Steve Mc - Queen, un - der - neath ___ your ra - dar screen, ___

you'll nev-er catch ___ us to-night. ___ Oh!

you'll nev-er catch ___ me to-night. ___

Additional Lyrics

I ain't taking shit off no one,
Baby, that was yesterday.
I'm an all American rebel
Making my big getaway.
Yeah, you know it's time,
I gotta fly.

A CHANGE WOULD DO YOU GOOD

Words and Music by SHERYL CROW,
JEFF TROTT and BRIAN McLEOD

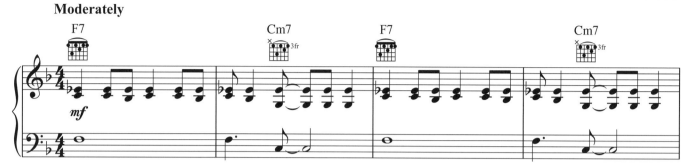

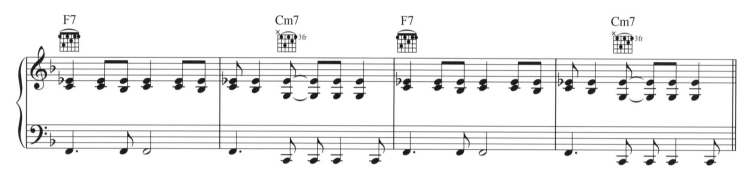

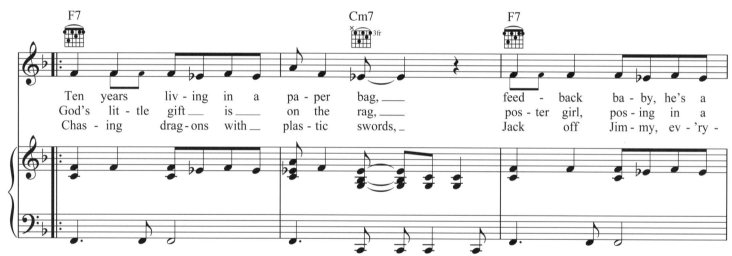

Ten years liv-ing in a pa-per bag, ___ feed-back ba-by, he's a
God's lit-tle gift ___ is ___ on the rag, ___ pos-ter girl, pos-ing in a
Chas-ing drag-ons with ___ plas-tic swords, _ Jack off Jim-my, ev-'ry-

flipped-out cat. ___ He's a plat-'num ca-nar-y, drink-in' Fal-staff beer, ___
fash-ion mag. ___ Ca-nine, ___ fe-line, ___ Je-kyll and Hyde?
bod-y wants more. Scul-ly and an-gel on the kit-chen floor, ___ and

Copyright © 1996 Reservoir 416, Warner-Tamerlane Publishing Corp., Weenie Stand Music, ole Red Cape Songs and Trottsky Music
All Rights for Reservoir 416 Administered Worldwide by Reservoir Media Management, Inc.
All Rights for Weenie Stand Music Administered by Warner-Tamerlane Publishing Corp.
All Rights for ole Red Cape Songs and Trottsky Music Administered by Anthem Entertainment
All Rights Reserved   Used by Permission

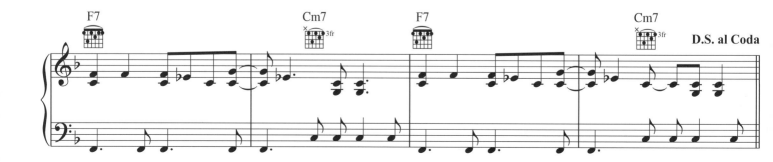

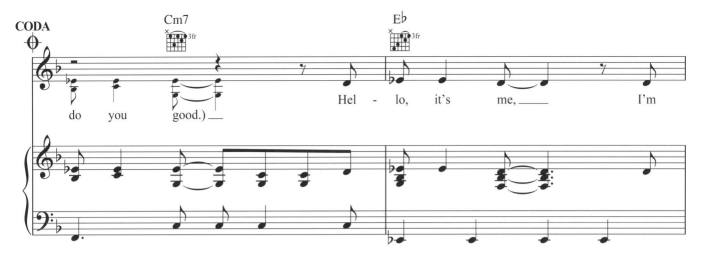

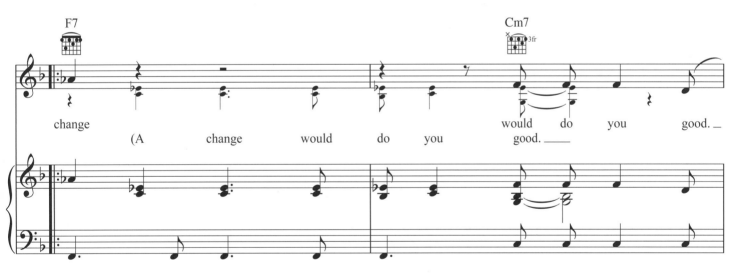

HOME

Words and Music by
SHERYL CROW

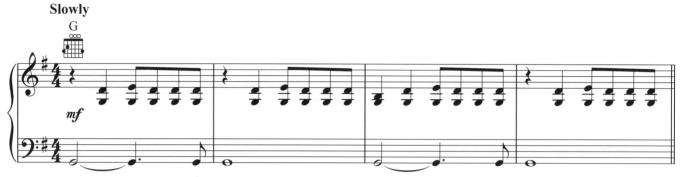

I woke up this morn - ing, now I un - der - stand
I found you stand - ing there when I was sev - en - teen. Now I'm
I'm go - ing cra - zy a lit - tle ev - 'ry day. And

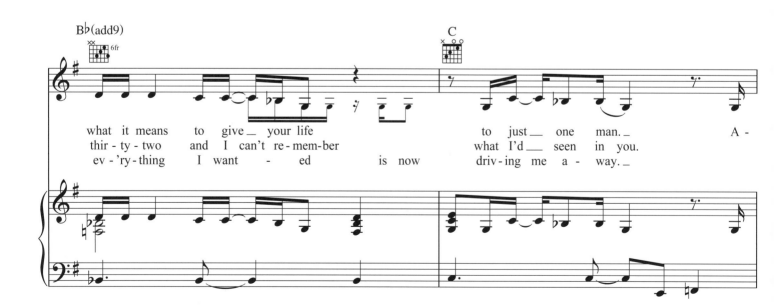

what it means to give your life to just one man. A-
thir - ty - two and I can't re - mem - ber what I'd seen in you.
ev - 'ry - thing I want - ed is now driv - ing me a - way.

Copyright © 1996 Reservoir 416
All Rights Administered Worldwide by Reservoir Media Management, Inc.
All Rights Reserved   Used by Permission

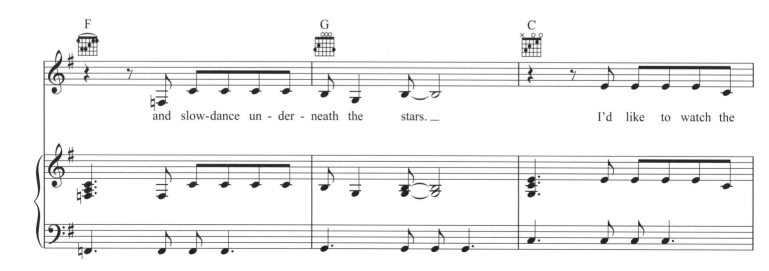

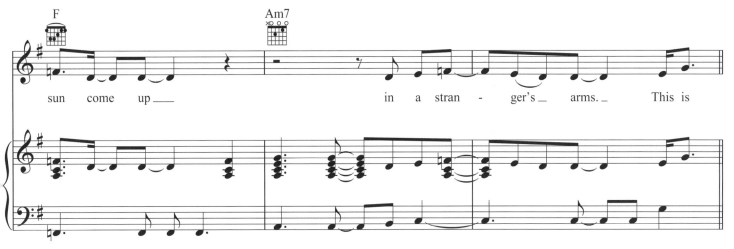

sun come up ____ in a stran - ger's ____ arms. ____ This is

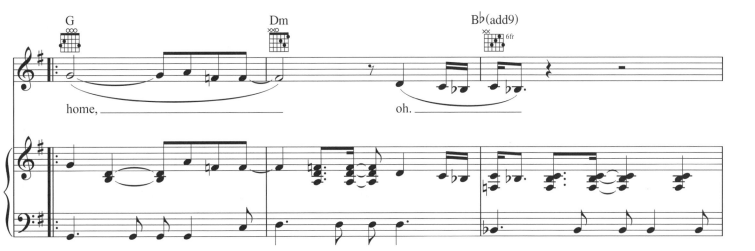

home, ____ oh. ____

(Sung 2nd time) Home, ____

home. ____ And this is ____

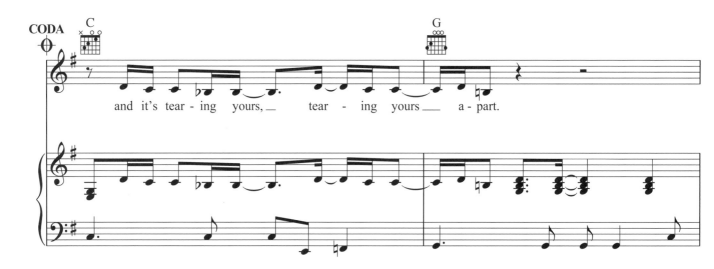

and it's tear-ing yours, __ tear - ing yours __ a-part.

And it's tear-ing yours __ a-part. __ Tear-ing yours __ a-part, __

and it's tear-ing us __ a-part. __

Repeat and Fade

I SHALL BELIEVE

Words and Music by SHERYL CROW
and BILL BOTTRELL

Copyright © 1993 Reservoir 416 and Ignorant Music
All Rights for Reservoir 416 Administered Worldwide by Reservoir Media Management, Inc.
All Rights for Ignorant Music Administered by Downtown DLJ Songs
All Rights Reserved   Used by Permission

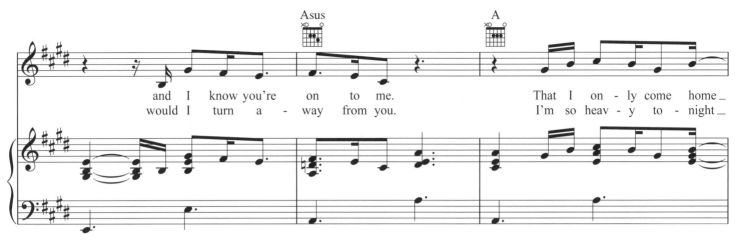

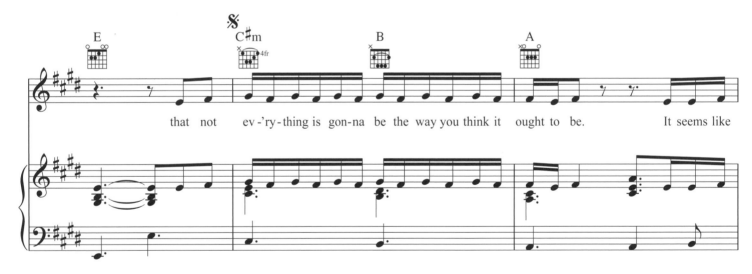

give up on me ____ and I shall be - lieve.

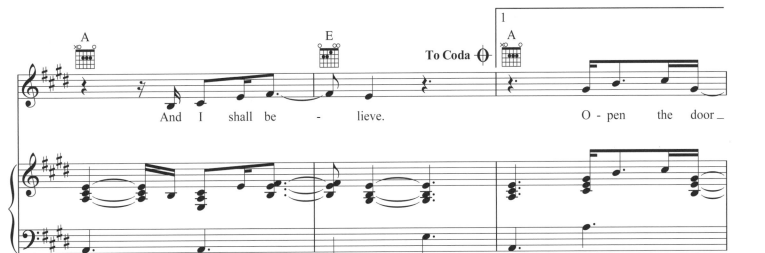

And I shall be - lieve. O - pen the door ____

____ And I shall be - lieve.

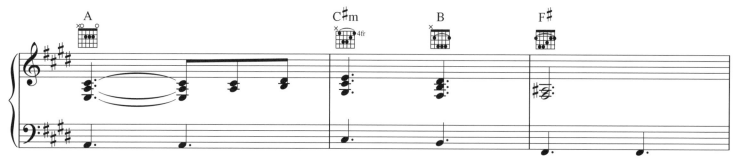

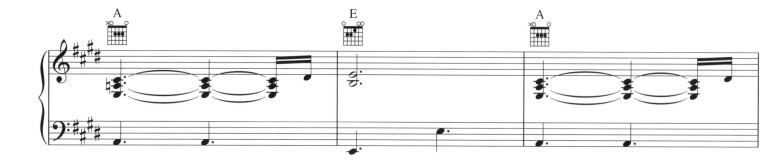

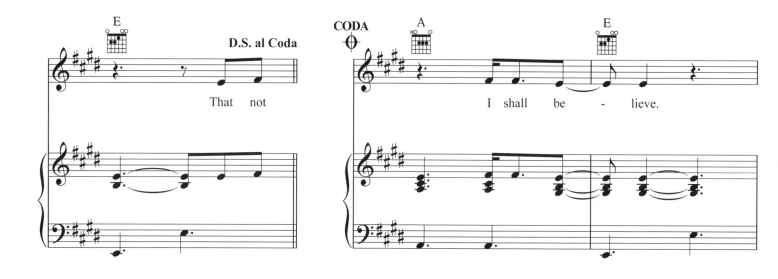

D.S. al Coda

That not

CODA

I shall be - lieve.

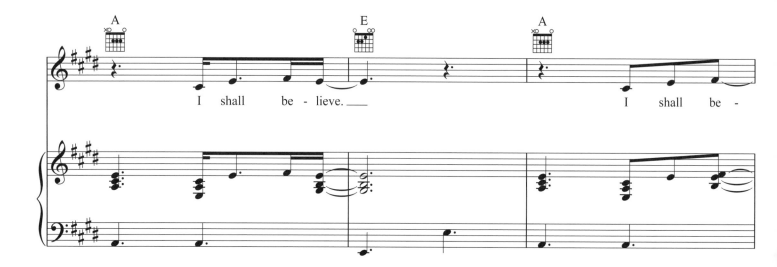

I shall be - lieve. ____

I shall be -

THERE GOES THE NEIGHBORHOOD

Words and Music by SHERYL CROW
and JEFF TROTT

Moderate Rock

Hey, let's par - ty, let's get down, __ let's turn the ra - di - o on this is the melt-
chick made to look sick - ly is stand - ing in her pant - ies in the show-

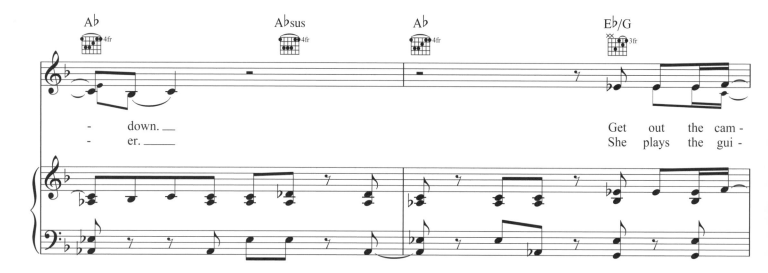

- down. __
- er. ____

Get out the cam-
She plays the gui-

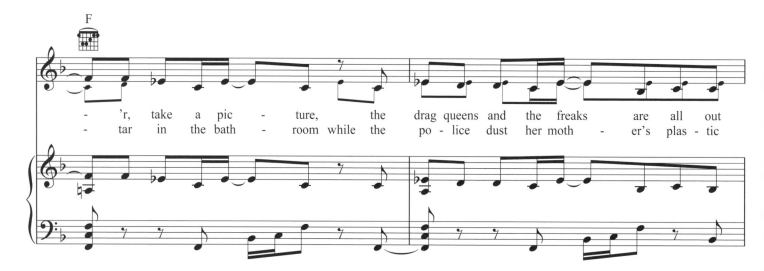

- 'r, take a pic - ture, the drag queens and the freaks are all out
- tar in the bath - room while the po - lice dust her moth - er's plas - tic

Copyright © 1998 Reservoir 416, ole Red Cape Songs and Trottsky Music
All Rights for Reservoir 416 Administered Worldwide by Reservoir Media Management, Inc.
All Rights for ole Red Cape Songs and Trottsky Music Administered by Anthem Entertainment
All Rights Reserved Used by Permission

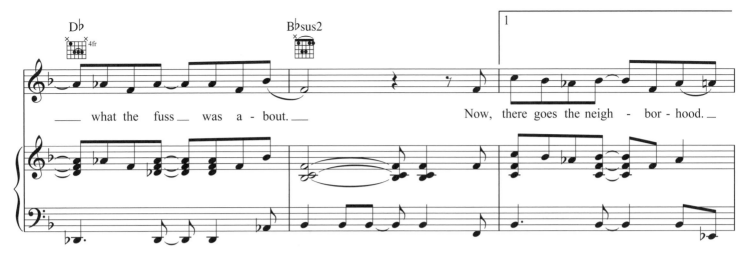

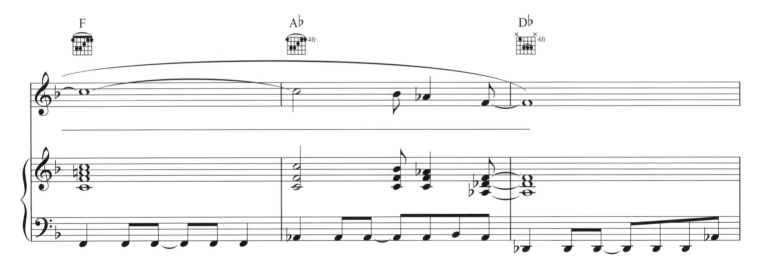

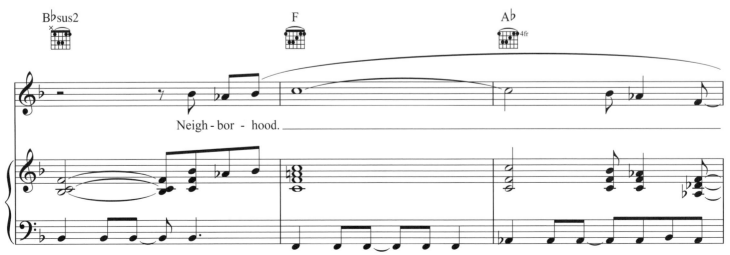

Now, there goes the neigh - bor - hood. __

This is the mov-

-ie of the screen - play of the book ___ a - bout __ a girl ___ who meets a junk-

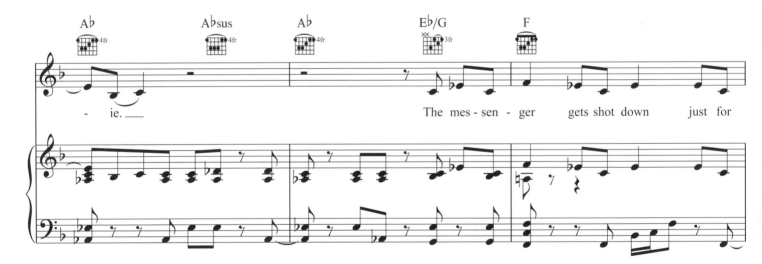

- ie. ___ The mes - sen - ger gets shot down just for

car - ry - ing ___ the mes - sage to a flunk - ie. ___

We can't be cer - tain who the vil - lains are __ 'cuz ev-'ry - one's __ so

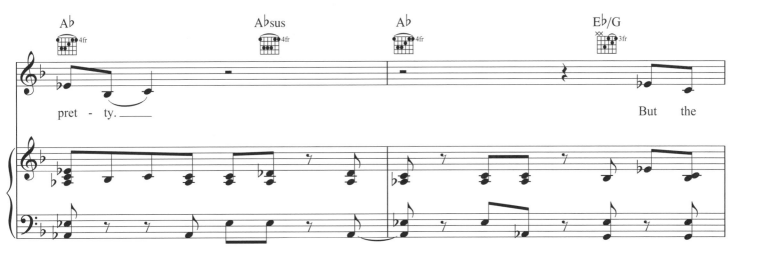

pret - ty. _____   But the

af - ter par - ty's sure   to   be __   a wing - ding, as   it moves in - to your __

D.S al Coda

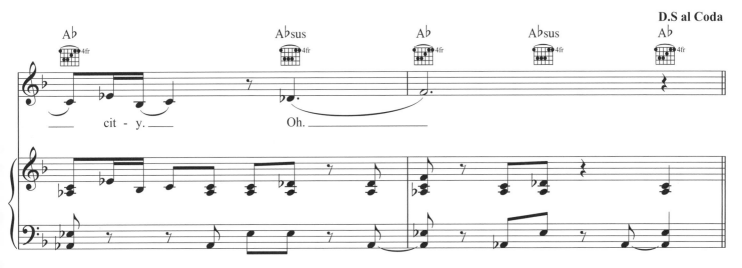

__ cit - y. __   Oh. _____

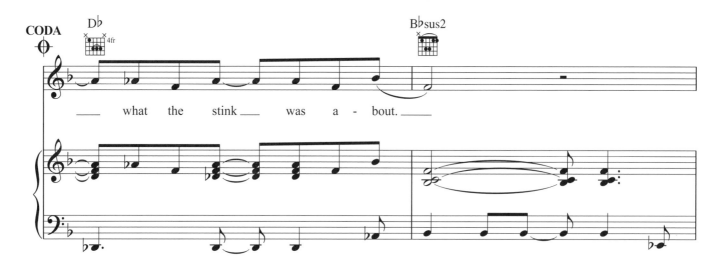

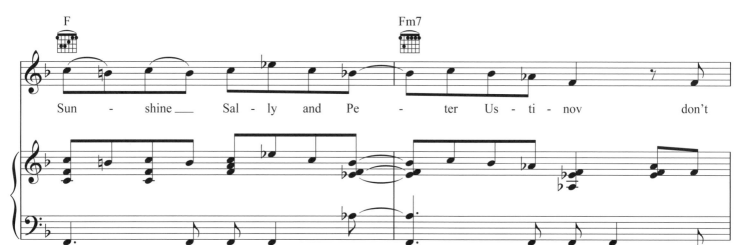

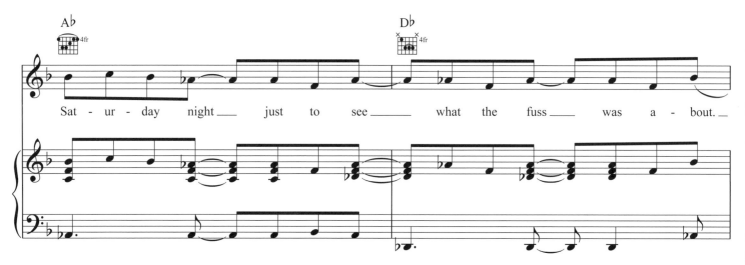

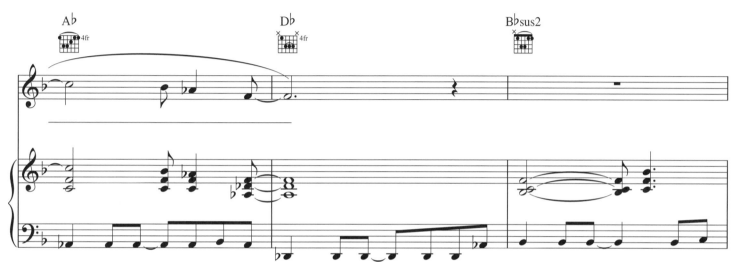